Verse by Verse Commentary on

PHILIPPIANS

AND

COLOSSIANS

Enduring Word Commentary Series

By David Guzik

The grass withers, the flower fades,
but the word of our God stands forever.
Isaiah 40:8

Commentary on Philippians and Colossians

Copyright ©2019 by David Guzik

Printed in the United States of America
or in the United Kingdom

Print Edition ISBN: 1-56599-029-3

Enduring Word

5662 Calle Real #184

Goleta, CA 93117

Electronic Mail: ewm@enduringword.com

Internet Home Page: www.enduringword.com

Scripture references, unless noted, are from the New King James Version of the Bible, copyright ©1979, 1980, 1982, Thomas Nelson, Inc., Publisher.

Contents

*Dedicated to
Jan Guzik*

Philippians 1 - Paul's Love and Concern for the Philippians

A. Paul's greeting to the Philippian Christians and his prayer for them.

1. (1-2) Address and initial greeting.

Paul and Timothy, bondservants of Jesus Christ, To all the saints in Christ Jesus who are in Philippi, with the bishops and deacons: Grace to you and peace from God our Father and the Lord Jesus Christ.

a. **Paul and Timothy**: The Apostle Paul wrote this letter to his close friends, the Christians in Philippi, from his Roman house arrest described at the end of Acts (Acts 28:30-31) as he waited for his court appearance before Caesar (around the year A.D. 61).

b. **To all the saints in Christ Jesus who are in Philippi**: The church in **Philippi** was founded by Paul some eleven years before this letter on his second missionary journey (Acts 16:11-40). This was the first church established on the continent of Europe.

c. **To all**: Paul addressed the letter to three groups.

- **To all the saints in Christ Jesus**: This means all the Christians in Philippi. **All** Christians *are* **saints**, but *only* in **Christ Jesus**.

- To **the bishops**: In a general sense, this meant those with leadership responsibilities. The ancient Greek word meant *overseers* and was used to describe general leadership before it came to describe a specific *office* recognized by some Christian traditions.

- To the **deacons**: Those who had recognized positions of *service*.

d. **Grace to you and peace**: Paul gave his familiar greeting of **grace** and **peace**, recognizing that these come to us only from God our Father and through the Son.

2. (3-6) Paul gives thanks for the Philippian Christians.

I thank my God upon every remembrance of you, always in every prayer of mine making request for you all with joy, for your fellowship in the gospel from the first day until now, being confident of this very thing, that He who has begun a good work in you will complete *it* until the day of Jesus Christ;

a. **I thank my God upon every remembrance of you**: When Paul remembered what all the Philippians did for him, he was extremely thankful. He was naturally grateful to the Philippians, but more so to **God** who had worked such kindness through the Philippians.

i. The Philippians were extremely giving towards Paul, both when he was with them (Acts 16:15, 16:32-34) and when he was apart from them (2 Corinthians 8:1-7, 9:1-4, and 11:9).

b. **Making request for you all**: Paul prayed for the Philippians and he did so with **joy**. This was one way Paul felt he could repay the Philippians for all they did for him.

i. One might simply say that when Paul prayed for the Philippians, he became happy. It is remarkable to see that Paul's first reference to his own feelings or frame of mind in this letter is that of **joy** – though he wrote from prison and a possible soon execution.

ii. "It is a glorious revelation of how life in fellowship with Christ triumphs over all adverse circumstances. The triumph, moreover, is not that of stoical indifference. It is rather the recognition of the fact that all apparently adverse conditions are made allies of the soul and ministers of victory, under the dominion of the Lord." (Morgan)

iii. "This is Paul's great singing letter. It was at Philippi that he had sung in prison at midnight, in the company of Silas. Now he was again in prison, this time in Rome." (Morgan)

c. **For your fellowship in the gospel**: This was one reason Paul was thankful for the Philippians. The idea is that the Philippians "partnered" with Paul in his spreading of the gospel through their friendship and financial support, and they did so **from the first day until now**. They didn't wait to see if Paul was a "winner" before they supported him. They got behind Paul and his ministry early.

d. **He who has begun a good work in you will complete it until the day of Jesus Christ**: When Paul thought of the beginning of God's work among the Philippians (**from the first day**), it was natural that he also thought of the day when that work would be **complete**. Paul also expressed his *confidence* in God's ability to complete that work.

i. It was indeed a **good work** begun in the Philippians and in all believers. "The work of grace has its root in the divine goodness of the Father, it is planted by the self-denying goodness of the Son, and it is daily watered by the goodness of the Holy Sprit; it springs from good and leads to good, and so is altogether good." (Spurgeon)

ii. Because this **good work** was begun, Paul was confident of its *completion*. God is a worker who completes His works. "Where is there an instance of God's beginning any work and leaving it incomplete? Show me for once a world abandoned and thrown aside half formed; show me a universe cast off from the Great Potter's wheel, with the design in outline, the clay half hardened, and the form unshapely from incompleteness." (Spurgeon)

iii. This work in the believer will not be finally complete until **the day of Jesus Christ**, which in context has the idea of the second coming of Jesus and our resurrection with Him. "Holy Scripture does not regard a man as perfect when the soul is perfected, it regards his body as being a part of himself; and as the body will not rise again from the grave till the coming of the Lord Jesus, when we shall be revealed in the perfection of our manhood, even as he will be revealed, that day of the second coming is set as the day of the finished work which God hath begun." (Spurgeon)

3. (7-8) Paul declares his affection for the Philippians.

Just as it is right for me to think this of you all, because I have you in my heart, inasmuch as both in my chains and in the defense and confirmation of the gospel, you all are partakers with me of grace. For God is my witness, how greatly I long for you all with the affection of Jesus Christ.

a. **It is right for me to think this of you all**: Paul's thankfulness, joy, and desire to pray for the Philippians was right because they stood beside him in his trials for the gospel, and they received the same grace he did (**you all are partakers with me of grace**).

b. **I have you in my heart**: Paul was a man of towering intellect, but he was also a man of great **heart**, and the Philippian Christians were in his **heart**. He could even call God as his **witness** regarding his deep **affection** for them.

i. Adam Clarke paraphrased Paul's idea here: "I call God to witness that I have the strongest affection for you, and that I love you with that same kind of tender concern with which Christ loved the world when he gave himself for it."

4. (9-11) Paul's prayer for the Philippians.

And this I pray, that your love may abound still more and more in knowledge and all discernment, that you may approve the things that are excellent, that you may be sincere and without offense till the day of Christ, being filled with the fruits of righteousness which *are* by Jesus Christ, to the glory and praise of God.

a. **This I pray, that your love may abound still more and more**: The Philippians had a lot of love, and they showed it to Paul. Yet Paul didn't hesitate to pray that their love would **abound still more and more**. It doesn't matter how much love for others we have; we can still have more!

i. "That it may be like a river, perpetually fed with rain and fresh streams so that it continues to swell and increase until it fills all its banks, and floods the adjacent plains." (Clarke)

b. **That your love may abound still more and more in knowledge and all discernment**: Yet, the love Paul wanted to abound in the Philippians was not "blind love." It was love that had **knowledge and all discernment**; it was love that could **approve the things that are excellent**.

i. Paul knew the danger of an undiscerning love. He rebuked the Corinthian church that seemed to glory in their "love" and "openness" which lacked any sense of knowledge and discernment (1 Corinthians 5:1-7).

c. **That you may be sincere and without offense**: When we approve and receive **the things that are excellent**, we become **sincere** (speaking of *inner* righteousness) **and without offense** (speaking of *outer* righteousness that can be seen). **Till the day of Christ** means that these things become increasingly evident in our life until Jesus comes.

i. Being **sincere** is important, but alone it is not enough. Notorious sinners in the days of Jesus such as tax collectors were sincere, yet they still needed to repent. As well, being **without offense** before others is important, but alone it is not enough. The Pharisees of Jesus' day were without offense in the opinion of many. We want God to make us *both* **sincere** and **without offense**.

d. **Being filled with the fruits of righteousness**: The work of becoming **sincere and without offense** is really God's work within us. It happens as we are **filled with the fruits of righteousness**.

i. Bearing fruit is always the result of abiding in Jesus (John 15:4-6). As we abide in Him, we receive the life and nutrients we need to naturally bear fruit **to the glory and praise of God**.

ii. "Every genuine follower of God has his glory in view by all that he does, says, or intends. He loves to glorify God, and he glorifies him by showing forth in his conversion the glorious working of the glorious power of the Lord." (Clarke)

B. Paul explains his present circumstances.

1. (12-14) Paul's imprisonment has not hindered the gospel in any way.

But I want you to know, brethren, that the things *which happened* to me have actually turned out for the furtherance of the gospel, so that it has become evident to the whole palace guard, and to all the rest, that my chains are in Christ; and most of the brethren in the Lord, having become confident by my chains, are much more bold to speak the word without fear.

a. **The things which happened to me have actually turned out for the furtherance of the gospel**: Paul here answered a concern of the Philippians. He wanted them to know that God's blessing and power were still with him, even though he was in prison. He was not out of the will of God, and God's work still continued.

i. When Paul was with the Philippians, there were amazing examples of the sovereign power of God, culminating in a divine jail-break and their vindication before civil magistrates (Acts 16:11-40). We are not surprised that the Philippians wondered where the power of God was in Paul's *present* imprisonment.

ii. We also know that all this turned out **for the furtherance of the gospel** because during this time he wrote Ephesians, Philippians, and Colossians.

iii. God didn't waste Paul's time during the Roman imprisonment. God never wastes our time, though we may waste it by not sensing God's purpose for our lives at the moment.

b. **The furtherance of the gospel**: Paul doesn't mention if *he* was being advanced, because he didn't care about that and he assumed that the Philippians didn't care either. Their common passion was the **furtherance of the gospel**, and the gospel continued to advance.

c. **It has become evident to the whole palace guard, and to all the rest, that my chains are in Christ**: The circumstances around Paul's imprisonment and his manner in the midst of it made it clear to all observers that he was not just another prisoner, but that he was an emissary of Jesus Christ. This witness led to the conversion of many, even some of the **palace guard**.

i. From this we see that Paul could minister effectively and bring glory to God in less than ideal circumstances. He didn't need everything to be easy and set in order to be fruitful.

d. **Having become confident by my chains**: Paul's imprisonment gave the Christians around him - who were not imprisoned - greater confidence and boldness.

- They saw that Paul had *joy* in the midst of such a trial.
- They saw that God would *take care* of Paul in such circumstances.
- They saw that God could still *use* Paul even when he was imprisoned.

2. (15-18) Paul considers the motives of others in their preaching.

Some indeed preach Christ even from envy and strife, and some also from good will: The former preach Christ from selfish ambition, not sincerely, supposing to add affliction to my chains; but the latter out of love, knowing that I am appointed for the defense of the gospel. What then? Only *that* in every way, whether in pretense or in truth, Christ is preached; and in this I rejoice, yes, and will rejoice.

a. **Some indeed preach Christ even from envy and strife**: Paul knew that some preached because they wanted to "surpass" Paul in ministry and to promote their own name and place above Paul's.

i. These people were *glad* Paul was imprisoned because they felt this gave them a competitive edge over him in what they considered to be the contest of preaching the gospel. They were motivated - at least in part - by a competitive spirit, which too often is common among preachers.

ii. Paul wasn't so critical or cynical to believe that *every* other preacher had bad motives. He knew that **some also** preached **from good will**.

b. **The former preach Christ from selfish ambition**: Those preaching the gospel out of wrong motives are infected with **selfish ambition**, which makes them serve, but **not sincerely**.

i. **Ambition** isn't necessarily bad; there is nothing wrong in wanting to be the best we can be for God. But *selfish* ambition is most concerned about a successful *image*, instead of striving for true success before God.

c. **Supposing to add affliction to my chains**: Those who preached Christ from the wrong motive supposed **to add affliction to** Paul's **chains**. Their competitive hearts didn't only want to win for themselves; they also wanted Paul to lose.

i. They wanted Paul to admit the humiliation of having to admit that others were more effective in ministry than he was. They didn't understand that Paul honestly didn't care about this, because he did not have a competitive spirit in ministry.

ii. A.W. Tozer wrote this powerful piece rebuking the attitude of competition that is common among those in the ministry: "Dear Lord, I refuse henceforth to compete with any of Thy servants. They have congregations larger than mine. So be it. I rejoice in their success. They have greater gifts. Very well. That is not in their power nor in mine. I am humbly grateful for their greater gifts and my smaller ones. I only pray that I may use to Thy glory such modest gifts as I possess. I will not compare myself with any, nor try to build up my self-esteem by noting where I may excel one or another in Thy holy work. I herewith make a blanket disavowal of all intrinsic worth. I am but an unprofitable servant. I gladly go to the foot of the cross and own myself the least of Thy people. If I err in my self- judgment and actually underestimate myself I do not want to know it. I purpose to pray for others and to rejoice in their prosperity as if it were my own. And indeed it is my own if it is Thine own, for what is Thine is mine, and while one plants and another waters it is Thou alone that giveth the increase." (from *The Price of Neglect*, 104-105)

d. **Only that in every way, whether in pretense or in truth, Christ is preached; and in this I rejoice, yes, and will rejoice**: So, people preached the gospel more energetically, motivated by Paul's imprisonment. Some were motivated in a good way and some were motivated in a bad way; yet nonetheless, they were *motivated* - and Paul could **rejoice** in that.

i. Remember that Paul's concern here was *not* with the *content* of the gospel being preached, only with the *motives* of those who preached. Paul objected if he thought a false or distorted gospel was preached, even if from the best of motives (Galatians 1:6-9).

ii. Paul's attitude went like this: "If you preach the true gospel, I don't care what your motives are. If your motives are bad, God will deal with you - but at least the gospel is preached. But if you preach a false gospel, I don't care how good your motives are. You are dangerous and must stop preaching your false gospel, and good motives don't excuse your false message."

iii. If Paul's imprisonment could not hinder the gospel, neither could the wrong motives of some. God's work was still getting done, and that was cause for rejoicing.

3. (19-20) Paul's confidence in his present circumstances.

For I know that this will turn out for my deliverance through your prayer and the supply of the Spirit of Jesus Christ, according to my earnest expectation and hope that in nothing I shall be ashamed, but with all boldness, as always, so now also Christ will be magnified in my body, whether by life or by death.

a. **I know that this will turn out for my deliverance**: Paul knew that the Lord was in control of all events, even though his imprisonment and impending trial before Caesar Nero made the situation look pretty dark.

b. **Through your prayer**: Paul was so confident because he knew that the Philippians prayed for him. His **deliverance** in the present situation was connected to the **prayer** of the Philippians.

i. We can hypothetically say that if the Philippians *didn't* pray for Paul, then God's deliverance for Paul would be hindered. It certainly seems that Paul thought this way, and it shows what a serious matter prayer is.

c. **Through your prayer and the supply of the Spirit of Jesus Christ**: However, it was not the prayer of the Philippians in and of itself that would meet Paul's need. It was the **supply of the Spirit of Jesus Christ** that came to Paul **through** the prayer of the Philippians. Paul's needs were met by the Spirit of God, but this provision to Paul was brought about by the prayers of the Philippians.

d. **My earnest expectation and hope**: These are words of faith. Paul mightily trusted God here, and Paul first trusted God **that in nothing I shall be ashamed**. He believed that God would not cause him to be **ashamed** or that God would not turn against him in the matter.

i. Though he was in prison and awaiting trial before Caesar, Paul had the confidence that he was in the center of God's will. He knew God was not punishing him through the adversity he experienced at the time.

e. **Christ will be magnified in my body, whether by life or by death**: Paul also had this trust, and admitted to the Philippians that he might not be released from this present imprisonment, but it might instead result in his martyrdom.

i. Paul lived his life not to preserve and promote himself, but to glorify Jesus Christ. If Jesus should one day decide that Paul could best glorify Him through laying down his life, then Paul would be well pleased by the opportunity.

ii. Even so, this must have hit hard on the Philippians who saw God do so many remarkable miracles of deliverance in Paul's life among them in Philippi (Acts 16:11-40). It would have been easy for the Philippians to associate God's glory only with being delivered *from* one's problems, not in being delivered in the *midst* of one's problems.

iii. It is easy for us to dictate to God *how* He can and cannot glorify Himself in our lives. Paul wisely left all that up to God.

4. (21-26) Paul's lack of fear regarding death and how it affected his outlook on ministry.

For to me, to live *is* Christ, and to die *is* gain. But if *I* live on in the flesh, this *will mean* fruit from *my* labor; yet what I shall choose I cannot tell. For I am hard pressed between the two, having a desire to depart and be with Christ, *which is* far better. Nevertheless to remain in the flesh *is* more needful for you. And being confident of this, I know that I shall remain and continue with you all for your progress and joy of faith, that your rejoicing for me may be more abundant in Jesus Christ by my coming to you again.

a. **For to me, to live is Christ, and to die is gain**: Paul knew that death was not a defeat to the Christian. It is merely a graduation to glory, a net **gain** for the Christian.

i. Paul's death at the time would be a **gain** in two senses.

- First, his death for the cause of Christ would glorify Jesus, and that was **gain**.
- Second, to be in the immediate presence of the Lord was **gain** for Paul.

ii. The idea that Paul could consider death a present **gain** argues against the idea of "soul sleep." This false teaching says that the believing dead are held in some sort of suspended animation until the resurrection occurs. His understanding that his death might be considered **gain** also argues against the idea of "purgatory" which says that the believing dead must be purified through suffering before coming into the presence of God.

iii. This also obviously showed that Paul did not *fear* death. Though some men may fear *dying*, no Christian should fear *death*. "When men fear death it is not certain that they are wicked, but it is quite certain that if they have faith it is in a very weak and sickly condition." (Spurgeon)

b. **But if I live on in the flesh, this will mean fruit from my labor**: Paul was confident that God intended him to be fruitful. There was no doubt in Paul's mind that this was God's plan for him. If Paul lived, it would be a fruitful life.

i. In sad contrast, many Christians have not yet come to the place where it is a certainty that they will bear fruit for the kingdom of God with their life.

c. **For I am hard pressed between the two**: Knowing that his death could be a gain - both for the gospel and for him personally - Paul was torn between being with the Lord or continuing to minister to the Philippians and others.

d. **Having a desire to depart and be with Christ**: It is strong to say, but one must say that Paul, in some way, *wanted to die*. In fact, **desire** describes a strong longing: "He said he had a desire to depart, and the desire was a strong one. The Greek word has much force in it. He panteth, he longeth to be gone." (Spurgeon)

i. Other men have also wanted to die.

- Some men have wished to die, gripped by the gloom and darkness that leads to suicide.

- Some have been so tired of this world and the cruelty of others that they thought death was better.

- Some have wanted to die in the crisis of some kind of suffering.

ii. Paul's **desire to depart** had nothing in common with these attitudes among men. Paul probably had many motivations to depart.

- Going to heaven meant he would finally be done with sin and temptation.

- Going to heaven meant that he would see those brothers and sisters who had gone to heaven before him.

- Most of all, going to heaven meant being **with Christ** in a closer and better way than ever before.

iii. **Having a desire to depart**: "It appears to be a metaphor taken from the commander of a vessel, in a foreign port, who feels a strong desire, to set sail, and get to his own country and family; but this desire is counterbalanced by a conviction that the general interests of the voyage may be best answered by his longer stay in the port where his vessel now rides; for he is not in dock, he is not aground, but rides at anchor in the port, and may any hour weigh and be gone." (Clarke)

iv. Paul knew that if he did **depart**, the journey would not be long. "The sail is spread; the soul is launched upon the deep. How long will be its voyage? How many wearying winds must beat upon the sail ere it shall be reefed in the port of peace? How often shall that soul be tossed upon the waves before it comes to the sea that knows no storm. Oh tell it, tell it everywhere; yon ship that has just departed is already at its haven. It did but spread its sail and it was there." (Spurgeon)

e. **Nevertheless to remain in the flesh is more needful for you**: Paul understood that others still needed him; that his work was not yet done. So while allowing for the possibility of his martyrdom, he told the Philippians that he *expects* to be spared at this time (**I know that I shall remain and continue with you**).

i. Paul was **confident** and full of faith, yet seems short of absolute certainty. His lack of absolute certainty is a comfort to us. Even the great apostle did not have a prophet's certainty about the future.

ii. As it happened, Paul survived this imprisonment, was set free, and was martyred later at Rome. He did come to visit the Philippians again.

f. **That your rejoicing for me may be more abundant in Jesus Christ by my coming to you again**: Paul's friendship with the Philippians was so close that he knew that they would be **rejoicing** to see him again.

C. How the Philippians should act in Paul's absence.

1. (27) Paul wanted the Philippians to work together for the cause of the gospel.

Only let your conduct be worthy of the gospel of Christ, so that whether I come and see you or am absent, I may hear of your affairs, that you stand fast in one spirit, with one mind striving together for the faith of the gospel,

a. **Only let your conduct**: The ancient Greek word translated "**conduct**" means literally, "to live as a citizen." Paul told the Philippians to be good, patriotic citizens of the kingdom of God. This is a theme he will draw on again in Philippians.

b. **I may hear of your affairs**: Paul wanted the Philippians to know they were accountable before him. He would check up on them.

c. **That you stand fast in one spirit, with one mind**: Paul wanted to know that the Philippian church stayed together as one body, without becoming fragmented and fractionalized.

d. **Striving together for the faith of the gospel**: Paul wanted their unity to be put to a productive purpose, so that an increasing trust and belief in the good news of Jesus Christ would be promoted among those who already believed and among those who had yet to believe.

2. (28) Paul wants the Philippians to be bold before their adversaries.

And not in any way terrified by your adversaries, which is to them a proof of perdition, but to you of salvation, and that from God.

a. **And not in any way terrified by your adversaries**: In the ancient Greek language, **terrified** "is a vivid term, unique in the Greek Bible and denoting the uncontrollable stampede of startled horses." (Martin) In the face of this kind of opposition, Paul wanted the Philippian Christians to have the same kind of boldness he had.

b. **Which is to them a proof of perdition**: When Christians are **not in any way terrified by** [their] **adversaries**, that in itself is **proof of perdition** - meaning *destruction* - to their adversaries.

i. **Perdition** (the ancient Greek word *apolia*) means *destruction, wasting,* or *damnation.* The word is also used in places like Philippians 3:19 and 2 Peter 2:1. Both Judas (John 17:12) and the Antichrist (2 Thessalonians 2:3) are called the *son of perdition.*

ii. When Christians stand strong against intimidation against the world, the flesh and the devil, it shows those spiritual enemies that their ultimate destruction is certain.

iii. When our spiritual enemies fail to make us afraid, they have failed completely because they really have no other weapon than fear and intimidation.

iv. When we *fail* to be **not in any way terrified by our adversaries**, we give "hope" and "confidence" to our spiritual enemies, even though it is a false hope and confidence because their destruction is still assured.

c. **But to you of salvation**: When Christians are **not in any way terrified by** [their] **adversaries**, it is also evidence of their own **salvation**. In the Lord, we can surprise ourselves with our boldness.

3. (29-30) Why the Philippians need not be terrified by their adversaries: the attacks and challenges they face are ordained by God.

For to you it has been granted on behalf of Christ, not only to believe in Him, but also to suffer for His sake, having the same conflict which you saw in me and now hear *is* in me.

a. **For to you it has been granted**: It was **granted** to the Philippians to **believe in Him**. In the same way this belief was **granted** to them, so also was the privilege to **suffer for His sake**.

i. The Philippians didn't need to fear that their present trial (and Paul's present trial) meant that God abandoned them. Their present difficulty was **granted** to them, not as a punishment, but as a tool in God's hand.

b. **But also to suffer for His sake**: The ancient Greek word for **suffer** here is *pasko*. This word is used primarily in the sense of persecution. However, it is also used of physical sufferings not related to persecution (Acts 28:5, and Matthew 17:15), of suffering under temptation (Hebrews 2:18) and hardships in a general sense (1 Corinthians 12:26, and Galatians 3:4).

i. "Everyone cannot be trusted with suffering. All could not stand the fiery ordeal. They would speak rashly and complainingly. So the Master has to select with careful scrutiny the branches which can stand the knife." (Meyer)

ii. "Look up and take each throb of pain, each hour of agony, as a gift. Dare to thank Him for it. Look inside the envelope of pain for the message it enfolds. It is a rough packing-case, but there is treasure in it." (Meyer)

c. **Having the same conflict which you saw in me and now hear is in me**: The Philippians had the same kind of **conflict** Paul had among them in Philippi and the same kind that Paul faced in Rome. The **conflict** of the Philippians concerned the difficulty of walking right with the Lord and proclaiming the gospel when persecuted and under attack.

i. **Conflict** is the ancient Greek word *agon*, which described a place where athletic contests were held and later came to refer to the contest itself. We get our words *agony* and *agonize* from this ancient Greek word.

ii. If the Philippians had Paul's kind of **conflict**, they could also have Paul's kind of joy and fruit in the midst of it.

Philippians 2 - Humble Living In Light of Jesus' Humble Example

A. How Paul wants the Philippians to live with each other.

1. (1) The basis of Paul's exhortation to the Philippians.

Therefore if *there is* any consolation in Christ, if any comfort of love, if any fellowship of the Spirit, if any affection and mercy,

> a. **Therefore**: This draws back to what Paul has built on in Philippians 1:27-30, telling the Philippians how to stand strong for the Lord against *external* conflicts. Now he tells them how to act against *internal* conflicts in the body of Christ.

> b. **If there is any**: This introduces the *basis* for Paul's exhortation to unity, humility and love among believers. The idea is that if the Philippian Christians have received the things he mentions, then they have a responsibility to do what he is about to describe.

> > i. "It is extremely difficult to give the force of these expressions; they contain a torrent of most affecting eloquence; the apostle pouring out his whole heart to a people whom with all his heart he loved, and who were worthy of the love even of an apostle." (Clarke)

> c. **If there is any consolation in Christ**: Paul asked this as a rhetorical question, knowing of course that there was great **consolation in Christ**. Every Christian should know the **consolation** of **Christ**.

> > i. Luke 2:25 says that one of the titles for Jesus as the Messiah is *the Consolation of Israel*. Paul could say in 2 Corinthians 1:5, *For as the sufferings of Christ abound in us, so our consolation also abounds through Christ*. In 2 Thessalonians 2:16, Paul says that God *has loved us and given us everlasting consolation and good hope by grace*. Of course there is **consolation in Christ**!

18

ii. "The Holy Spirit consoles, but Christ *is the consolation*. If I may use the figure, the Holy Spirit is the Physician, but Christ is the medicine." (Spurgeon)

d. **If there is any... comfort of love**: This is Paul's second rhetorical question in this passage, affirming the great **comfort of love**. Every Christian should know what it is to have Jesus give him the **comfort of love**.

i. 2 Corinthians 1:3 says that God is the *God of all comfort*. There is no way He cannot comfort us and no circumstance beyond His comfort. But this is more than comfort; this is the **comfort of love**.

ii. The word **comfort** in this passage is the ancient Greek word *paraklesis*. The idea behind this word for **comfort** in the New Testament is always more than soothing sympathy. It has the idea of strengthening, of helping, of making strong. The idea behind this word is communicated by the Latin word for **comfort** (*fortis*), which also means "brave." The love of God in our life makes us strong and makes us brave. Of course there is **comfort of love**!

e. **If there is any... fellowship of the Spirit**: This is Paul's third rhetorical question in this context. Paul knew and valued the **fellowship of the Spirit**, and every Christian should know what it is to have the **fellowship of the Spirit**.

i. **Fellowship** is the ancient Greek word *kononia*. It means the sharing of things in common. We share life with the Spirit of God that we never knew before. The Holy Spirit fills and guides and moves in our lives in a powerful and precious way. Of course there is **fellowship of the Spirit**!

ii. "The Lord doth usually and graciously water the holy fellowship of his people with the dews of many sweet and glorious refreshings; so that they have a very heaven upon earth." (Trapp)

f. **If there is any... affection and mercy**: Paul's final rhetorical question assumes that every Christian knows something of the **affection** of God and of the **mercy** of God.

i. Paul mentioned these things in a manner that suggests to us that they should all be obvious parts of the Christian's experience. To make his rhetorical point, he could have just as easily said, "If water is wet, if fire is hot, if rocks are hard," and so forth.

ii. Each of these gifts – **consolation in Christ, comfort of love, fellowship of the Spirit, affection and mercy** – are communicated to us both in a direct, spiritual way from Jesus, and from Jesus *through His* *people.* But there isn't any doubt that these are real gifts for Christians to really experience.

2. (2-4) The specifics of Paul's exhortation to the Philippians regarding love and humility among believers.

Fulfill my joy by being like-minded, having the same love, *being* of one accord, of one mind. *Let* nothing *be done* through selfish ambition or conceit, but in lowliness of mind let each esteem others better than himself. Let each of you look out not only for his own interests, but also for the interests of others.

a. **Fulfill my joy**: This speaks of a personal request. Part of the reason Paul wanted the Philippians to take heed to his word was because they should know that it would make the founding apostle of their church happy.

b. **By being like-minded, having the same love, being of one accord, of one mind**: These together all speak of the same idea: a deep, abiding, internal unity among the Philippians.

i. This unity is the goal. What follows in Philippians 2:3-4 are descriptions of how to achieve and practice the unity mentioned here in Philippians 2:2.

c. **Let nothing be done through selfish ambition**: This is the first step to this kind of unity. In the flesh, we are often motivated by **selfish ambition** or **conceit**. Much of what we do is not done out of love for others, but out of our own desire for "advancement" or "promotion" (**selfish ambition**).

i. Paul found it important to say *selfish* **ambition**. Not all ambition is *selfish* ambition, and there is a *good* **ambition** to glorify God and serve Him with everything we have.

d. **Let nothing be done through... conceit**: This is the second step to this kind of unity. **Conceit** is thinking too highly of one's self, of having an excessive self-interest and self-preoccupation. It could be more literally translated "empty glory."

i. A dictionary definition of **conceit** is "An excessively favorable opinion of one's own ability, importance, wit," and so forth. When we live with the feeling that we are so important, or so able, or so talented, we are out of God's will. We are working against the unity Paul pleaded with the Philippians and all Christians to have.

e. **In lowliness of mind let each esteem others better than himself**: This third step to the kind of unity described in Philippians 2:2 is completely contradictory to the attitude of the world, because **lowliness of mind** is about the least attractive thing to the thinking of this world.

i. The ancient Greeks considered **lowliness of mind** to be a fault, not a virtue. "The pagan and the secular idea of manhood is self-assertiveness, imposing one's will on others; when anyone stooped to others he did so only under compulsion, hence his action was ignominious [disgraceful]. The Christian ethical idea of humility could not be reached by the secular mind; it lacked the spiritual soil." (Lenski)

ii. "In pagan writers generally, the word had a bad meaning, 'abject, grovelling.' But when it comes into the New Testament, its meaning is ennobled." (Wuest)

iii. "The apostle knew that, to create concord, you need first to beget lowliness of mind. Men do not quarrel when their ambitions have come to an end." (Spurgeon)

f. **Esteem others better than himself**: This rebukes much of the culture's concept of self-esteem. The Bible knows nothing of the idea that we should - and must - carry with us an attitude of confident superiority in every situation, and knows nothing of the idea that this is the foundation for a healthy human personality.

i. While we recognize the intrinsic value of every human life, we can't deny that the low self-esteem of some is *justified*, and based in *reality*. When we are in rebellion against God, it is fitting for us to have a low self-esteem.

ii. As we **esteem others better**, we will naturally have a concern for their needs and concerns. This sort of *outward* looking mentality naturally leads to a unity among the people of God.

iii. If I consider you above me and you consider me above you, then a marvelous thing happens: we have a community where everyone is looked up to, and no one is looked down on.

g. **Let each of you look out not only for his own interests, but also for the interests of others**: Here the thought is completed. As we put away our selfish ambitions, our conceit, and our tendencies to be high-minded and self-absorbed, we will naturally have a greater concern for the interests and needs of others.

i. Paul doesn't tell us that it is wrong to **look out** for our own interests, but that we should not *only* look out for our own interests.

B. Jesus, the ultimate example of humility.

Many regard Philippians 2:5-11 as a hymn of the early church that Paul incorporated into his letter. Some commentators go so far as to suggest stanza and verse arrangements for the "hymn." This is possible, but not a necessary conclusion;

Paul was capable of such inspired, poetic writing himself (example: 1 Corinthians 13). For reasons which we will examine later, this passage is often known as the kenosis *passage.*

1. (5) Paul applies the lesson before he states it.

Let this mind be in you which was also in Christ Jesus,

a. **Let this mind be in you which was also in Christ Jesus**: Paul will, in wonderful detail, describe for us the **mind** of Jesus in the following verses. But here, before he describes the mind of Jesus, he tells us what we must *do* with the information.

i. "Paul does not give all that is in the mind of Christ in these verses. He selects those qualities of our Lord which fit the needs of the Philippians at that moment.... This lack of unity among the Philippian saints became the occasion for perhaps the greatest Christological passage in the New Testament that sounds the depths of the incarnation." (Wuest)

b. **Let this mind be in you**: It is all too easy for us to read the following description of Jesus and admire it from a distance. God wants us to be awed by it, but also to see it as something that we must enter into and imitate. **Let this mind** means that it is something that we have *choice* about.

i. Remember also that this **mind** is something granted to us by God. 1 Corinthians 2:16 says that *we have the mind of Christ*. But **let this mind** shows us that it is also something we must *choose* to walk in. You have to **let** it be so.

2. (6a) Jesus was **in the form of God**.

Who, being in the form of God,

a. **In the form of God**: This describes Jesus' pre-incarnate existence. We must remind ourselves that Jesus did not begin His existence in the manger at Bethlehem, but is eternal God.

b. **Being**: This is from the ancient Greek verb *huparchein*, which "describes that which a man is in his very essence and which cannot be changed. It describes that part of a man which, in any circumstances, remains the same." (Barclay)

i. "Paul, by the use of the Greek word translated 'being,' informs his Greek readers that our Lord's possession of the divine essence did not cease to be a fact when He came to earth to assume human form.... *This word alone is enough to refute the claim of Modernism that our Lord emptied Himself of His Deity when He became Man.*" (Wuest)

c. **Form**: This translates the ancient Greek word *morphe*. It "always signifies a form which truly and fully expresses the being which underlies it... the words mean 'the being on an equality with God.'" (Expositors)

> i. "*Morphe* is the essential form which never alters; *schema* is the outward form which changes from time to time and from circumstance to circumstance." (Barclay)

> ii. "'God' has a form, and 'Jesus Christ' exists in this form of God." (Lenski)

> iii. Wuest explains that the ancient Greek word translated **form** is very difficult to translate. When we use the word **form**, we think of the *shape* of something; but the ancient Greek word had none of that idea. It is more the idea of a *mode* or an *essence*; it is the essential nature of God, without implying a physical shape or image. "Thus the Greek word for 'form' refers to that outward expression which a person gives of his inmost nature."

3. (6b) Jesus did not cling to the privileges of deity.

Did not consider it robbery to be equal with God,

a. **Did not consider it robbery**: The ancient Greek in this phrase has the idea of something being grasped or clung to. Jesus did not cling to the prerogatives or privileges of deity.

> i. Wuest defines the ancient Greek word translated **robbery** as, "A treasure to be clutched and retained at all hazards."

b. **To be equal with God**: It wasn't that Jesus was trying to *achieve* equality with the Father. He *had it,* and chose not to cling to it. Jesus' divine nature was not something He had to seek for or acquire, but it was His already.

> i. Lightfoot wrote that it was not "a prize which must not slip from His grasp, a treasure to be clutched and retained at all hazards." Jesus was willing to let go of some of the prerogatives of deity to become a man.

4. (7) Jesus made Himself of **no reputation**.

But made Himself of no reputation, taking the form of a bondservant, *and* coming in the likeness of men.

a. **But made Himself of no reputation**: The more common (and well-known) translation of this is that *He emptied Himself.* From the ancient Greek word *emptied* (*kenosis*) came the idea that Jesus' incarnation was essentially a self-emptying.

i. We must carefully think about what Jesus *emptied* Himself of. Paul will tell us plainly in the following verses, but we must take care that we do not think that Jesus emptied Himself of His deity in any way.

ii. Some develop the *kenotic theory* of the incarnation to the point where they insist that Jesus divested Himself of many of the attributes of deity - such as omniscience, omnipotence, omnipresence, and even suffered the elimination of His own divine self-consciousness. Yet Jesus did not (and *could* not) become "less God" in the incarnation. No deity was *subtracted* (though he did renounce some of the rights of deity); rather humanity was *added* to His nature.

iii. "During his humiliation, as God and equal with the Father, was no encroachment on the Divine prerogative; for, as he had an *equality* of *nature*, he had an *equality* of *rights*." (Clarke)

iv. "His condescension was free, and unconstrained with the consent of his Father... the Son of the Highest can, at his own pleasure, show or eclipse his own glorious brightness, abate or let out his fullness, exalt or abase himself in respect of us." (Poole)

v. "Even as a king, by laying aside the tokens of his royalty, and putting on the habit of a merchant, when all the while he ceaseth not to be a king, or the highest in his own dominions." (Poole)

b. **Taking the form of a bondservant**: This describes *how* Jesus emptied Himself. Though he took **the form of a bondservant**, Jesus did not empty Himself of His deity, or of any of His attributes, or of His equality with God. He emptied Himself *into* the form of a **bondservant**, not merely the form of a man.

i. **Taking** (the ancient Greek word *labon*) does not imply an *exchange*, but an *addition*.

c. **Coming in the likeness of men**: This further describes how Jesus emptied Himself. We can think of someone who is a servant, but not in the **likeness of men**. Angels are servants, but not in the **likeness of men**. In fairy tales, Aladdin's genie was a servant, but not in the **likeness of men**.

i. The word for **likeness** here *may* refer to merely the outward form of something. While Jesus did have the outward form of humanity, the outward form reflected His true humanity, which was added to His deity.

ii. "It was a likeness, but a real likeness, no mere phantom humanity as the Docetic Gnostics held." (Robertson)

5. (8) The extent of Jesus' self-emptying.

And being found in appearance as a man, He humbled Himself and became obedient to *the point of* death, even the death of the cross.

a. **He humbled Himself and became obedient**: Jesus **humbled Himself** when He **became obedient**. This was something that Jesus could only experience by coming down from the throne of heaven and becoming a man. When God sits enthroned in heaven's glory, there is no one He obeys. Jesus had to leave heaven's glory and be **found in appearance as a man** in order to become **obedient**.

i. One key to Jesus' obedience on earth was the endurance of suffering. This again was something He could only learn by experience after the incarnation. As it is written: *though He was a Son, yet He learned obedience by the things which He suffered* (Hebrews 5:8).

ii. Indeed, **He humbled Himself**.

- He was humble in that he took the form of a man, and not a more glorious creature like an angel.
- He was humble in that He was born into an obscure, oppressed place.
- He was humble in that He was born into poverty among a despised people.
- He was humble in that He was born as a child instead of appearing as a man.
- He was humble in submitting to the obedience appropriate to a child in a household.
- He was humble in learning and practicing a trade – and a humble trade of a builder.
- He was humble in the long wait until He launched out into public ministry.
- He was humble in the companions and disciples He chose.
- He was humble in the audience He appealed to and the way He taught.
- He was humble in the temptations He allowed and endured.
- He was humble in the weakness, hunger, thirst, and tiredness He endured.
- He was humble in His total obedience to His Heavenly Father.
- He was humble in His submission to the Holy Spirit.

- He was humble in choosing and submitting to the death of the cross.

- He was humble in the agony of His death.

- He was humble in the shame, mocking, and public humiliation of His death.

- He was humble in enduring the spiritual agony of His sacrifice on the cross.

iii. We can imagine that it was possible for the Son of God to become man and pay for the sins of the world without this great humiliation. He might have added the humanity of a 33-year old man to his deity. He might have appeared before man only in His transfigured glory, and taught men what they needed to hear from Him. He might have suffered for the sins of man in a hidden place of the earth far from the eyes of man, or on the dark side of the moon for that matter. Yet He did not; **He humbled Himself**, and did it for the surpassing greatness of our salvation and His work for us.

b. **To the point of death, even the death of the cross**: This states the extent of Jesus' humility and obedience.

i. Crucifixion was such a shameful death that it was not permitted for Roman citizens (such as the people of Philippi). A victim of crucifixion was considered by the Jews to be particularly cursed by God (Deuteronomy 21:23 and Galatians 3:13).

ii. Robertson called the **death of the cross** "The bottom rung in the ladder from the Throne of God. Jesus came all the way down to the most despised death of all, a condemned criminal on the accursed cross."

iii. **Even the death of the cross** shows that there is no limit to what God will do to demonstrate His love and saving power to man; this was and forever will be the ultimate. "What must sin have been in the sight of God, when it required such abasement in Jesus Christ to make an atonement for it, and *undo* its influence and malignity!" (Clarke)

iv. "The lower he stoops to save us, the higher we ought to lift him in our adoring reverence. Blessed be his name, he stoops, and stoops, and stoops, and, when he reaches our level, and becomes man, he still stoops, and stoops, and stoops lower and deeper yet." (Spurgeon)

c. **Even the death of the cross**: All of this was a great display of the power of Jesus. Remember that because of Paul's past experience among the Philippians, they were tempted to think of God's *power* as being expressed only in exaltation and deliverance and not in terms of glorifying God through humble service and endurance.

i. In this, Paul reminded the Philippians that his current place of humble circumstances (his Roman imprisonment) could still show forth the glory and power of God, even as Jesus did in His humility.

C. Jesus, the ultimate example of exaltation after humility.

1. (9) The exaltation of Jesus Christ.

Therefore God also has highly exalted Him and given Him the name which is above every name,

a. **Therefore God has also highly exalted Him**: This is the general heading for the material in the next three verses. These words describe how God has exalted Jesus. Indeed, **highly exalted** could also be translated "super exalted."

i. "The Greek elegancy imports superexalted, or exalted with all exaltation." (Poole)

ii. "Now, just pause over this thought – that Christ did not crown himself, but that his Father crowned him; that he did not elevate himself to the throne of majesty, but that his Father lifted him there, and placed him on his throne." (Spurgeon)

b. **Given Him the name which is above every name**: This goes beyond giving Jesus the Divine name Yahweh. When we consider the Hebrew concept of **the name**, it also implies that God declares that Jesus has a *character* and *person* above all.

i. This verse, with its clear statement of Jesus' deity, is powerful ammunition against those who deny the deity of Jesus Christ. There is no higher name than Yahweh, and Jesus has that **name**.

2. (10-11) The subjection of the whole creation to Jesus.

That at the name of Jesus every knee should bow, of those in heaven, and of those on earth, and of those under the earth, and *that* every tongue should confess that Jesus Christ *is* Lord, to the glory of God the Father.

a. **That at the name of Jesus every knee should bow**: Not only is Jesus exalted by the Father, but the whole world is brought into submission to the Son.

i. "Paul does not imply by this a universal salvation, but means that every personal being will ultimately confess Christ's lordship, either with joyful faith or with resentment and despair." (Kent)

b. **Those in heaven, and of those on earth, and of those under the earth**: This conveys the absolute totality of all creation recognizing the superiority of Jesus Christ.

> i. In this, Paul draws on the idea of Isaiah 45:23: *I have sworn by Myself; the word has gone out of My mouth in righteousness, and shall not return, that to Me every knee shall bow, every tongue shall take an oath*. Notice that in Isaiah, it is to Yahweh that all knees bow and tongues confess. In Philippians it is to Jesus, showing that Jesus *is* Yahweh.

> ii. **Those under the earth**: "Either the dead, who are hid in the earth, and shall be raised by the power of Christ... or, devils, and wicked souls." (Poole)

c. **Every knee should bow... every tongue should confess**: The combination of **tongues confessing** and **knees bowing** gives evidence that the idea is a complete submission to Jesus, both in word and in action, and one that is required of all.

> i. The totality of this recognition of Jesus' deity and exaltation has caused many to envision this happening in a formal way after the final judgment, when every creature in heaven and hell is required to bow their knees and make the confession **that Jesus Christ is Lord**.

d. **That Jesus Christ is Lord**: From this we can say that there is a sense in which Jesus *returned* to heaven with more than He had than when He *left* heaven. Not only did He return with His humanity still added to his deity (although a resurrected humanity), He also returned with the recognition planted among men of who He was and the worship He deserved - something unknown until the Incarnation and the full revelation of His person and work.

> i. "He has always (in Paul's view) shared in the Divine nature. But it is only as the result of His Incarnation, Atonement, Resurrection and Exaltation that He *appears to men* as on an equality with God, that He is *worshipped by them* in the way in which Jehovah is worshipped." (Expositors)

> ii. "He might have used the miraculous powers inherent in His Divine nature in such a way as to compel men, without further ado, to worship Him as God. Instead of that He was willing to attain this high dignity by the path of humiliation, suffering and death." (Expositors)

> iii. All this must be seen in reference to the humiliation described in Philippians 2:6-8; our tendency is to long for the exaltation, but to forsake the humiliation.

e. **Jesus Christ is Lord**: The confession of Jesus Christ as **Lord** reminds us to consider the great significance of this word *kurios*, especially as it was understood by the early church, who used the LXX as their Bible - where *kurios* was consistently used to translate the tetragrammaton, standing for the name *Yahweh*.

i. We also should not miss the significance that at a later time in the Roman Empire, all residents of the Empire were required to swear an oath of allegiance to the Emperor, declaring that *Caesar is Lord*, and burning a pinch of incense to an image of the emperor. Though the Roman state saw this only as a display of political allegiance, Christians rightly interpreted it as idolatry - and refused to participate, often paying with their lives.

ii. Paul has no doubt who is really Lord - not the Caesar whom he will stand trial before; *Caesar* may be a high name, but it is not the name above all names, the name which belongs to Jesus Christ!

f. **Jesus Christ is Lord, to the glory of God the Father**: Remember that Paul did not give this description of Jesus in Philippians 2:5-11 simply for the theological education of the Philippians.

- He gave it to equip them to endure the hardship they were experiencing.
- He gave it help them to understand Paul's hardships.
- He gave it to help them to practice real Christian unity in the midst of hard times.

i. This picture of Jesus has helped them to understand how to assess the ministry of Paul, which seemed weak at the present time.

ii. This picture helped them to understand the context of God's revelation of power - how God delights to show His power through humble actions.

iii. This picture has equipped them to act in a way towards each other that will promote unity in the body of Christ.

iv. This picture has shown them how to follow Jesus' pattern of patient, humble obedience - something Paul will call them to continue in the following verses.

D. Paul's exhortation to the Philippians.

1. (12) Working out your own salvation.

Therefore, my beloved, as you have always obeyed, not as in my presence only, but now much more in my absence, work out your own salvation with fear and trembling;

a. **Therefore... as you have always obeyed**: We should not miss the connection between the obedience *Jesus showed* (Philippians 2:8) and the obedience *Paul expected* of Christians as followers of Jesus (Philippians 2:12).

b. **Work out your own salvation**: We know that Paul did *not* mean "work so as to earn your own salvation." Such a statement would contradict the whole of Paul's gospel. What Paul *did* mean is to call the Philippians to put forth real effort into their Christian lives. This is not to **work** their salvation in the sense of accomplishing it, but to **work out** their salvation - to see it evident in every area of their lives, to *activate* this salvation God freely gave them.

i. Therefore, "These words, as they stand in the New Testament, contain no exhortation to all men, but are directed to the people of God. They are not intended as an exhortation to the unconverted; they are, as we find them in the epistle, beyond all question addressed to those who are already saved through a living faith in the Lord Jesus Christ." (Spurgeon)

c. **Work out your own salvation**: There is a sense in which our salvation is complete, in the sense that Jesus has done a complete work *for* us. Still there is also a sense in which our salvation is incomplete, in that it is not yet a complete work *in* us.

i. "The believer must finish, must carry to conclusion, must apply to its fullest consequences what is already given by God in principle... He must *work out* what God in His grace has *worked in*." (Muller)

ii. "Some professors appear to have imbibed the notion that the grace of God is a kind of opium with which men may drug themselves into slumber, and their passion for strong doses of sleepy doctrine grows with that which it feeds on. 'God works in us,' say they, 'therefore there is nothing for us to do.' Bad reasoning, false conclusion. God works, says the text; therefore we must work out because God works in." (Spurgeon)

iii. "He exhorts as if he were an Arminian in addressing men. He prays as if he were a Calvinist in addressing God and feels no inconsistency in the two attitudes. Paul makes no attempt to reconcile divine sovereignty and human free agency, but boldly proclaims both." (Robertson)

d. **Your own salvation**: This tells us to give attention to our **own salvation**. Sometimes we show great concern for the work of God in others, and not enough for His work in us. We should care about the souls of others, but this care must begin with our own soul.

e. **With fear and trembling**: Paul's idea was not that we should live our Christian lives with a constant sense of fear and terror, but that we should live with a fear of failing to **work out your own salvation**.

> i. We work out our salvation with **fear and trembling**; but it doesn't have to be the fear of hell or damnation. It may instead be the righteous and awe-filled reverence of God every believer should have. It doesn't have to be the **trembling** of a guilty sinner; it should instead be the joyful **trembling** of an encounter with the glory of God.

f. **Now much more in my absence**: In context, Paul asked for this Christian **work** ethic (not a *works* ethic) to be promoted all the more because of his **absence**.

2. (13) God's work in you.

For it is God who works in you both to will and to do for *His* good pleasure.

a. **For it is God who works in you**: Paul here gave the reason *why* Christians must *work out their salvation with fear and trembling* - because **God** is working in them.

> i. We take comfort in it: **God who works in you**. "Grace all-sufficient dwells in you, believer. There is a living well within you springing up; use the bucket, then; keep on drawing; you will never exhaust it; there is a living source within." (Spurgeon)

b. **God... works in you**: The idea is that since God has done and is doing a work in the Christian, the Christian therefore has a greater responsibility to work diligently with fear and trembling regarding his own salvation and walk with the Lord. God's work in us *increases* our responsibility; it doesn't *lessen* it in any way.

> i. Those that take God's sovereignty and working and use them as an excuse for inaction and lethargy are like the wicked and lazy servant of Matthew 25:24-30.

> ii. Those that are really God's servants use their understanding of His sovereignty and omnipotence as a motivation for greater, more dedicated service to Him.

c. **Both to will and to do**: God's work in us extends to the transformation of our **will**, as well as changing our actions (**to do**). Yet in light of the original exhortation to *work out your own salvation*, this is not a passive transaction.

d. **For His good pleasure**: This is the motive behind God's work in our life. He does so because it gives Him **pleasure** to do it.

3. (14-16) Practical ways to obey Paul's exhortation.

Do all things without complaining and disputing, that you may become blameless and harmless, children of God without fault in the midst of a crooked and perverse generation, among whom you shine as lights in the world, holding fast the word of life, so that I may rejoice in the day of Christ that I have not run in vain or labored in vain.

a. **Do all things without complaining and disputing**: There is a good deal of dispute among commentators as to if this **complaining and disputing** refers to problems among the Philippians (such as mentioned in Philippians 2:1-4) or if this refers to their attitude towards God. Perhaps they resented God because of their present conflict (Philippians 1:27-30).

i. Because Paul specifically used terms that were used to describe Israel's complaining towards God during the Exodus, it is probably best to see the **complaining and disputing** as including their attitude towards God. Spurgeon gives three examples of things we must not murmur against:

- The Providence of God.
- One another.
- The ungodly world.

ii. In this command, the emphasis falls on the words **all things**, which is actually the first word of the verse in the ancient Greek text.

iii. "Dispute not with God; let him do what seemeth him good. Dispute not with your fellow Christians, raise not railing accusations against them. When Calvin was told that Luther had spoken ill of him, he said, 'Let Luther call me devil if he please, I will never say of him but that he is a most dear and valiant servant of the Lord.' Raise not intricate and knotty points by way of controversy." (Spurgeon)

b. **That you may become blameless and harmless, children of God without fault**: Through the display of a non-complaining spirit, we show ourselves to be true followers of God.

i. **Harmless** can have the thought of "pure" or "unalloyed." But the translation as *harmless* is also justified (it is the same word used in Matthew 10:16).

ii. "'Be ye blameless *and harmless*,' says the apostle. The Greek word might be translated 'hornless,' as if ye were to be creatures not only that do no harm, but *could not do any*; like sheep that not only *will not* devour, but *cannot* devour, for it were contrary to their nature; for they have no teeth with which to bite, no fangs with which to sting, no poison with which to slay." (Spurgeon)

c. **In the midst of a crooked and perverse generation**: This seems to refer back to Deuteronomy 32:5: *They have corrupted themselves; they are not His children, because of their blemish: A perverse and crooked generation.* Paul meant that modern Christians should not be like rebellious Israel, who were constantly **complaining and disputing** with God during the wilderness sojourn.

d. **Among whom you shine as lights in the world**: This is not an encouragement to do something; it is a simple statement of fact. Christians *are* **lights in the world**; the only question is, "How brightly do they shine?"

i. "Not *lights* merely, but **luminaries**, *heavenly bodies*. But this can hardly be satisfactorily given in an English version." (Alford)

ii. We are to fulfill our place **as lights in the world**:

- Lights are used to make things evident.
- Lights are used to guide.
- Lights are used as a warning.
- Lights are used to bring cheer.
- Lights are used to make things safe.

iii. Paul knew that the lights were in a bad place. Instead of excusing the lights for not shining, Paul knew that their position made it all the more important that they shine. Being in a dark place is a greater incentive to shine.

e. **Holding fast the word of life**: The phrase **holding fast** could also be translated *holding forth*. Both meanings are true and Paul could have meant it in this dual sense. We *hold fast* - in the sense of holding strong - **the word of life**, and we also *hold forth* **the word of life**.

f. **So that I may rejoice in the day of Christ that I have not run in vain or labored in vain**: The idea that Paul's work might some how end up to be in vain was a troublesome thought to him. He knew that his work really abided in *people*, so that if those people did not continue on strong with the Lord, there was a sense in which his own ministry was **in vain**.

g. **In the day of Christ**: Paul looked forward to **the day of Christ**, and on that day he wanted to see and to know that his work was fruitful. This was something he could only be assured of if the Philippians continued to walk with the Lord.

i. This is the true heart of a shepherd: to have few burdens for one's self, but many for others; to not be content with one's own relationship with God, but also longing to see others walking with the Lord.

4. (17-18) Paul as an example of his own exhortation.

Yes, and if I am being poured out *as a drink offering* on the sacrifice and service of your faith, I am glad and rejoice with you all. For the same reason you also be glad and rejoice with me.

a. **Poured out as a drink offering**: Paul here alluded to a practice among both Jews and pagans in their sacrifices. They often poured out wine (or sometimes perfume) either beside (as in the Jewish practice) or upon (as in the pagan practice) an animal that was sacrificed to God or pagan gods.

i. This is the **drink offering**, which accompanied another sacrifice, that is mentioned in Numbers 15:4-5 and 28:7.

ii. The grammar of **I am being poured out** is in the *present* tense. With this Paul indicated the possibility that his execution may be imminent.

b. **On the sacrifice and service of your faith**: The ancient Greek word translated **service** is *leutrogia*. It meant, "Service to God or His cause... any priestly action or sacred performance." (Muller) Therefore, in this verse we have a *sacrifice*, a *priest*, and an *accompanying libation* that makes the sacrifice even more precious.

i. Since **the sacrifice and service** were connected with the **faith** of the Philippians, it is best to see Paul's picture describing them as the "priests" and their faith as the "sacrifice," to which Paul added (and thereby enriched) his martyrdom as a drink offering.

c. **I am glad and rejoice... you also be glad and rejoice with me**: Paul looked forward to what might be his imminent martyrdom, and expected the Philippians to **be glad and rejoice with** him. Paul wasn't being morbid here, asking the Philippians to take joy in something as depressing as his death. Yet he did ask the Philippians to see his death as something that would bring glory to God. This is a theme repeated from Philippians 1:20.

i. Paul's life was going to be a sacrifice for Jesus Christ, either in life or in death. This was a source of gladness and joy for Paul, and he wants the Philippians to adopt the same attitude.

ii. Again, we come to the consistent theme of Philippians: *joy*. But this is joy based not on circumstances (quite the opposite, really), but based in the fact of a life totally committed to Jesus Christ.

E. Paul, Timothy, and Epaphroditus.

1. (19-22) Paul writes about Timothy and his soon anticipated visit.

But I trust in the Lord Jesus to send Timothy to you shortly, that I also may be encouraged when I know your state. For I have no one like-minded, who will sincerely care for your state. For all seek their own, not the things which are of Christ Jesus. But you know his proven character, that as a son with *his* father he served with me in the gospel.

a. **But I trust in the Lord**: This showed Paul's heart of true reliance upon the Lord. He wanted to see Timothy among the Philippians, but recognized that it would happen God's way and in God's timing.

b. **That I also may be encouraged when I know your state**: Paul didn't expect problems from the Philippians, as if they were one of his problem churches. Instead, he expected that he would be **encouraged when I know your state**.

i. Contrast this with the attitude Paul conveyed to the Corinthian church in 2 Corinthians 13:2-3. The Corinthian church had much worse problems than the Philippian church had.

c. **Who will sincerely care for your state**: When Paul sent Timothy, he sent his best, a man who showed a pastor's heart and had greater concern for his sheep than for himself.

i. Paul recognized just how rare this kind of heart was when he observed **all seek their own, not the things which are of Christ Jesus**.

2. (23-24) Paul repeats his desire to come to the Philippians in person, not only to send Timothy to them.

Therefore I hope to send him at once, as soon as I see how it goes with me. But I trust in the Lord that I myself shall also come shortly.

a. **I trust in the Lord that I myself shall also come shortly**: Perhaps Paul was being careful to avoid the accusation, "Paul wants to send Timothy because he really doesn't want to be here himself." He clearly told the Philippians that he also wanted to come.

3. (25-26) Paul writes about Epaphroditus and his coming to the Philippians.

Yet I considered it necessary to send to you Epaphroditus, my brother, fellow worker, and fellow soldier, but your messenger and the one

who ministered to my need; since he was longing for you all, and was distressed because you had heard that he was sick.

a. **I considered it necessary to send to you**: This undoubtedly meant that Epaphroditus took this letter to the Philippians. It seems that **Epaphroditus** came to Paul from the Philippians as a messenger and became sick while he was with Paul.

b. **My brother, fellow worker, and fellow soldier**: Paul gave these important titles to Epaphroditus. He was a man Paul valued as a partner in the work of ministry.

i. There are three special relationships here mentioned:

- **Brother** speaks of a relationship to be enjoyed.
- **Worker** speaks of a job to be done.
- **Soldier** speaks of a battle to be fought.

c. **Your messenger and the one who ministered to my need**: This means that Epaphroditus brought a gift of financial support from the Philippians to Paul (Philippians 4:18).

i. **Ministered** has in it the idea of a priestly service. When Epaphroditus brought the support money from the Philippians to Paul in Rome, he brought a *sacrifice*.

d. **Because you had heard that he was sick**: Epaphroditus was concerned because the Philippians learned of his sickness and worried about him. The return of Epaphroditus would give them peace of mind that their valued brother was in good condition.

i. It would also help Epaphroditus because **he was longing for you all and was distressed**. He greatly longed to see the Philippian Christians.

4. (27) Epaphroditus' sickness and his recovery.

For indeed he was sick almost unto death; but God had mercy on him, and not only on him but on me also, lest I should have sorrow upon sorrow.

a. **For indeed he was sick almost unto death**: The sickness of Epaphroditus was no small thing; it was **almost unto death**. Yet **God had mercy on him** and he recovered.

i. There is nothing in the text to indicate that this was a miraculous healing, but Paul still saw God's hand of mercy in Epaphroditus' recovery.

b. **Lest I should have sorrow upon sorrow**: God's mercy to Epaphroditus was also mercy to Paul. If Epaphroditus had died, Paul would have had

sorrow upon sorrow because a valued brother, worker, and soldier for Christ was no longer on this earth. He would also have **sorrow upon sorrow** because Epaphroditus became sick when he came on behalf of the Philippians to minister to Paul's material and spiritual needs while Paul was in prison in Rome.

5. (28-30) Paul's instructions to the Philippians on how to receive Epaphroditus as he returns to them.

Therefore I sent him the more eagerly, that when you see him again you may rejoice, and I may be less sorrowful. Receive him therefore in the Lord with all gladness, and hold such men in esteem; because for the work of Christ he came close to death, not regarding his life, to supply what was lacking in your service toward me.

a. **I sent him the more eagerly**: Paul was eager to re-unite the Philippians with their beloved brother Epaphroditus, and reminded the Philippians to give him proper recognition when he returned (**hold such men in esteem**).

i. Probably, the Philippians sent Epaphroditus not only as a messenger, but also to be a personal attendant to Paul on behalf of the Philippians. When illness prevented Epaphroditus from doing this, he may have seemed like a failure (perhaps even a malingerer) in the eyes of the Philippians. Paul assured them this was not the case; in fact, it was just the opposite - Epaphroditus served above and beyond the call of duty.

b. **Because for the work of Christ he came close to death**: It was **for the work of Christ** that Epaphroditus came **close to death**. Even though his **work** was mostly that of being a messenger and not anything particularly spiritual, it was still **the work of Christ**.

c. **Not regarding his life**: The willingness to put the **work of Christ** first and his own personal safety and concern second displayed the noble heart of Epaphroditus.

i. The ancient Greek phrase **not regarding his life** uses a gambler's word that meant to risk everything on the roll of the dice. Paul wrote that for the sake of Jesus Christ, Epaphroditus was willing to gamble everything.

ii. In the days of the Early Church there was an association of men and women who called themselves *the gamblers*, taken from this same ancient Greek word used in **not regarding his life**. It was their aim to visit the prisoners and the sick, especially those who were ill with dangerous and infectious diseases. Often, when a plague struck a city, the heathen threw the dead bodies into the streets and fled in terror.

But the *gamblers* buried the dead and helped the sick the best they could, and so risked their lives to show the love of Jesus.

iii. "It seems plain from this expression that Epaphroditus' illness was the consequence not of persecution but of over-exertion." (Lightfoot)

d. **To supply what was lacking in your service toward me**: Epaphroditus did this by actually *bringing* the support that the Philippians gave. There was a *lack* in all the Philippians' generosity and good intentions until the gift finally made its way to Paul's need.

i. We should have the heart that there is something **lacking** in our **service** until the job is done. We should not be satisfied with good intentions or a half-done job.

Philippians 3 - Leaving Law and Pressing On to Jesus

A. The futility of a relationship with God based on the principle of law.

1. (1-2) Warning against the influence of legalistic Jews.

Finally, my brethren, rejoice in the Lord. For me to write the same things to you *is* not tedious, but for you *it is* safe. Beware of dogs, beware of evil workers, beware of the mutilation!

a. **Finally**: This didn't mean that Paul was almost finished; Paul wrote here as many preachers speak. Yet we should expect some sort of transition in the letter with the word **finally**.

i. "Paul's 'finally' here is not the 'finally' of the present day preacher. He has another 'finally' in 4:8. He does not mean by this that he is about to close the letter. The words translated by the word 'finally' are literally 'as for the rest.'" (Wuest)

b. **Rejoice in the Lord**: This is a fitting theme for the whole letter. Paul shared with the Philippians the principle of being able to rejoice **in the Lord** - not in circumstances or in situations, but **in the Lord** who works all things together for good.

i. This abiding joy is fitting for the believer because it shows that we really do trust in a God whom we really believe is in control. When we believe this, it isn't any surprise that we are then filled with joy.

ii. **Rejoice in the Lord**: "The entire phrase may be the Christian equivalent of the Old Testament exclamation, *Hallelujah*." (Martin)

iii. "*It is a duty for us to cultivate this joy*. We must steadfastly arrest any tendency to murmur and complain; to find fault with God's dealings; or to seek to elicit sympathy. We must as much resist the temptation to depression and melancholy as we would to any form of sin." (Meyer)

c. **For me to write the same things to you is not tedious, but for you it is safe**: Paul assured the Philippians that he didn't mind reminding them of the same things because it was for their safety.

> i. Paul did not mind reminding them because he was passionately concerned about certain dangers, and he would speak out strongly against them. "This outburst is very remarkable, for its vehemence is so unlike the tone of the rest of the letter. That is calm, joyous, bright, but this is stormy and impassioned, full of flashing and scathing words." (Maclaren)

d. **Beware of dogs**: This was a harsh reference to the troublemaking legalists who attempted to deceive the Philippians. "**Dogs**" is exactly the term of contempt Jews would use against Gentiles. Paul said a lot by using this word against these Jewish-influenced legalists.

> i. Muller quoting Lightfoot: "The herds of dogs which prowl about Eastern cities, without a home and without an owner, feeding on the refuse and filth of the streets, quarreling among themselves, and attacking the passer-by, explain the applications of the image."

> ii. "We are bidden, therefore, to beware of men of a quarrelsome and contentious spirit, who under the guise of religion hide impure and unclean things; and who are not only defiled, but defiling in their influence." (Meyer)

e. **Beware of evil workers**: This describes both what these legalists *do* (working **evil**), but was also a word against their emphasis on righteousness with God by *works*. Paul would admit that they have a concern for works, but they were *evil* **workers**.

> i. **Evil workers**: "These people are the 'Cranks' of our Churches; they introduce fads and hobbies; they exaggerate the importance of trifles; they catch up ever new theory and vagary, and follow it to the detriment of truth and love." (Meyer)

f. **Beware of the mutilation**: Here is another harsh reference to the insistence of these Jewish legalists on requiring circumcision for Gentiles who wanted to become Christians. This was all done with the idea that someone must become a Jew *first* before they could become a Christian.

> i. "They did not deny that Jesus was the Messiah, or that His Gospel was the power of God unto salvation, but they insisted that the Gentile converts could only come to the fullness of Gospel privilege through the Law of Moses." (Meyer)

> ii. However, Paul did not see their insistence on circumcision as something beautiful or noble; he regarded it as an ugly example of

mutilation. Maclaren imagines Paul saying it like this: "I will not call them the circumcision, they have not been circumcised, they have only been gashed and mutilated, it has been a mere fleshly maiming."

iii. Martin on *the* **mutilation**: "By a pun, he mockingly calls it a mere cutting, *katatome, i.e.* mutilation of the body on a par with pagan practices forbidden in Leviticus 21:5."

2. (3-4) Paul defines the *true* circumcision.

For we are the circumcision, who worship God in the Spirit, rejoice in Christ Jesus, and have no confidence in the flesh, though I also might have confidence in the flesh. If anyone else thinks he may have confidence in the flesh, I more so:

a. **For we are the circumcision**: These Jewish legalists considered themselves the ones truly circumcised and right with God. But Paul declared that he and his followers were the *true* **circumcision**.

b. **Who worship God in the Spirit**: This defines the true circumcision. They **worship God in the Spirit**, as opposed to the fleshly and external worship emphasized by these legalists.

i. "The word 'worship' is the translation of the Greek word referring to the service of Jehovah by His peculiar people, the Jews. A Jew would be scandalized by the application of this word to a Gentile." (Wuest)

c. **Rejoice in Christ Jesus**: This also characterizes those of the true circumcision. Their joy is not found in their own ability to be justified by the law or by their law-keeping. Jesus and Jesus alone is their joy.

d. **Have no confidence in the flesh**: This is a third characteristic of the true circumcision. They do not trust in their own ability to be righteous before God through external works (**the flesh**), but their only confidence is in Jesus.

e. **I also might have confidence in the flesh... I more so**: Paul knew that he was more qualified to be justified by the keeping of the law than any of his present legalistic opponents were.

i. Curiously, often those who promote the idea of having confidence in the flesh are the same ones who are the least qualified to have such confidence. This is because of the principle Paul explains in Colossians 2:23 - *These things indeed have an appearance of wisdom in self-imposed religion, false humility, and neglect of the body, but are of no value against the indulgence of the flesh.*

3. (5-6) Paul's reasons why he might have confidence in the flesh.

Circumcised the eighth day, of the stock of Israel, *of* the tribe of Benjamin, a Hebrew of the Hebrews; concerning the law, a Pharisee; concerning zeal, persecuting the church; concerning the righteousness which is in the law, blameless.

a. **Circumcised the eighth day...** : Paul first listed four things that were his possessions by birth, all reasons why he might have confidence in the flesh.

- Paul was **circumcised the eighth day** in accordance with Leviticus 12:3.

- Paul was **of the stock of Israel**, a descendant of Abraham, Isaac, and Jacob; and therefore an heir to God's covenant with them.

- Paul was of **the tribe of Benjamin**, a distinguished tribe. Benjamin was distinguished by the fact that it gave Israel her first king, Saul (1 Samuel 9:1-2). It was the tribe that aligned itself with faithful Judah when Israel divided into two nations at the time of Rehoboam (1 Kings 12:21). It was also the tribe that had the city of Jerusalem within its boundaries (Judges 1:21).

- Paul was **a Hebrew of the Hebrews**. This contrasted him with the Jews who embraced Greek culture as it spread through the Mediterranean. In that time, many Jews became ashamed of their Jewishness and tried to live and act as much like Greeks as they could, sometimes even to the point of having their circumcision cosmetically restored or hidden so they could enjoy the Roman public baths without being noticed as Jews. In contrast, Paul was raised by his parents as **a Hebrew of the Hebrews**.

b. **Concerning the law**: Paul then listed three things that were his by personal choice and conviction, all reasons why he might have confidence in the flesh.

- Paul was **concerning the law, a Pharisee**. This tells us that among an elite people (the Jews), Paul was of an elite sect (the Pharisees), who were noted for their scrupulous devotion to the law of God. "There were not very many Pharisees, never more than six thousand, but they were the spiritual athletes of Judaism. Their very name means *The Separated Ones*. They had separated themselves off from all common life and from all common tasks in order to make it the one aim of their lives to keep every smallest detail of the Law." (Barclay) The concern that Pharisees had for keeping the law is reflected in passages like Matthew 23:23.

- **Concerning zeal, persecuting the church**. Paul was not merely an *intellectual* opponent of perceived heresies against Judaism; he was also an active fighter against them - even in his blindness to God. Paul's observation that the Jews of his day *have a zeal for God, but not according to knowledge* (Romans 10:2) was true of his own life before God confronted him on the road to Damascus.

- **Concerning the righteousness which is in the law, blameless**. This shows that Paul achieved the standard of righteousness which was accepted among the men of his day - though this standard fell short of God's holy standard. Because of how the law was interpreted and taught, there were those of that day who were deceived into thinking that they really were **blameless**, like the rich young ruler (Luke 18:18-23).

    i. In summary, if *anyone* could lay claim to pleasing God by law-keeping and the works of the flesh, it was Paul. He was far more qualified than his legalizing opponents were to make such a claim.

4. (7) Paul rejects all confidence in the flesh.

But what things were gain to me, these I have counted loss for Christ.

a. **These I have counted loss for Christ**: Any of the corrupting teachers Paul warned against would be proud to claim Paul's pedigree. Yet Paul made it plain: **these things I have counted loss for Christ**.

    i. "The word 'gain' is plural in the Greek, namely, 'gains.'... 'Loss' is singular. The various gains are all counted as one loss." (Wuest)

    ii. "He was skilled in spiritual arithmetic, and very careful in his reckoning. He cast up his accounts with caution, and observed with a diligent eye his losses and his gains." (Spurgeon)

b. **I have counted loss**: Paul **counted** these things loss. It wasn't so much that they were a loss by their very character, as much as he chose to *regard* them as **loss**.

    i. They were **counted loss** not so much because they were harmful to Paul, but because these things were ways in which Paul sought to please God in the energies of the flesh. Before Paul became a Christian, he thought all these things made him a success in the effort to please God by works.

    ii. We can say that Paul's attitude was the same that Jesus described in the parable of the pearl of great price (Matthew 13:45-46).

B. Paul's utter confidence in a living relationship with Jesus Christ.

1. (8) Paul's gain in Jesus Christ.

Yet indeed I also count all things loss for the excellence of the knowledge of Christ Jesus my Lord, for whom I have suffered the loss of all things, and count them as rubbish, that I may gain Christ

a. **Yet indeed I also count all things loss**: Paul did not only count his religious pedigree as a loss; he counted **all things loss** - but he counted them as a loss in view of **the excellence of the knowledge of Christ Jesus**.

i. **Yet indeed**: "The translation of five particles, which latter are literally translated, 'yea, indeed, therefore, at least, even,' and show the force and passion of Paul's conviction." (Wuest)

ii. It wasn't so much that those things were worthless in themselves, but compared to the greatness of **the excellence of the knowledge of Christ Jesus**, they really were nothing.

iii. Paul here put a *personal relationship with Jesus Christ* at the very center of the Christian's life. He joyfully accepted the loss of all other things for the greatness of this personal relationship.

iv. In Philippians 3:7 Paul said that he *counted*; in this verse he said **I also count**. This first counting was at his conversion; the second – some 30 years later – was in his Roman prison. After all he had experienced, he still counted it worthy to give everything up for the sake of following Jesus.

v. "After twenty years or more of experience Paul had an opportunity of revising his balance-sheet, and looking again at his estimates, and seeing whether or not his counting was correct. What was the issue of his latest search? How do matters stand at his last stocktaking? He exclaims with very special emphasis, 'Yea doubtless; and I count all things but loss for the excellency of the knowledge of Christ Jesus my Lord.'" (Spurgeon)

b. **For whom I have suffered the loss of all things**: This counting loss was not merely an internal spiritual exercise. Paul had indeed **suffered the loss of all things** that he might gain Christ.

i. This is demonstrated by the place and circumstances under which Paul wrote this letter – a Roman prison, where he truly could say that he had **suffered the loss of all things**.

c. **Count them as rubbish**: Paul here used strong language. Literally, Paul considered them as excrement - as dung; not only as worthless, but as offensive.

i. The ancient Greek word for **rubbish** had one of two uses. It could describe excrement from the body or table scraps that were fit only to be thrown to the dogs. We may suppose that Paul would be comfortable with either meaning in this context.

ii. "The word [**rubbish**] means the vilest dross or *refuse* of any thing; the worst excrement. The word shows how utterly insignificant and unavailing, in point of salvation, the apostle esteemed every thing but the Gospel of Jesus." (Clarke)

2. (9) The spiritual benefits of his gain in Jesus Christ.

And be found in Him, not having my own righteousness, which *is* from the law, but that which *is* through faith in Christ, the righteousness which is from God by faith;

a. **And be found in Him**: Because Paul was **in Him**, he could renounce his **own righteousness** and live by the **righteousness which is from God by faith**. The foundation for his spiritual life was in what Jesus had done for him and not in what he had done, was doing, or would do for Jesus in the future.

b. **The righteousness which is from God by faith**: Paul here exposed the great difference between the legal relationship stressed by his opponents and his personal connection with Jesus Christ. The difference is between living and trusting in your own righteousness and living and trusting in God's righteousness given **through faith in Christ**.

i. "He disowns his own righteousness as eagerly as other men disown their sins, and he highly esteems the righteousness which Christ has wrought out for us, which becomes ours by faith." (Spurgeon)

3. (10-11) Paul's experience of a personal relationship with Jesus.

That I may know Him and the power of His resurrection, and the fellowship of His sufferings, being conformed to His death, if, by any means, I may attain to the resurrection from the dead.

a. **That I may know Him**: This was the simple plea of Paul's heart. It was a plea unknown to the legalist, who must necessarily focus on his own performance and status to find some kind of peace with God. But Paul wanted Jesus, not self.

i. To know Jesus is not the same as knowing His historical life; it is not the same as knowing correct doctrines regarding Jesus; it is not the same as knowing His moral example, and it is not the same as knowing His great work on our behalf.

- We can say that we know someone because we recognize him: because we can distinguish what is different about him compared to other people.

- We can say that we know someone because we are acquainted with what he does; we know the baker because we get our bread from him.

- We can say that we know someone because we actually converse with him; we are on speaking terms with that person.

- We can say that we know someone because we spend time in his house and with his family.

- We can say that we know someone because we have committed our life to him and live with him every day, sharing every circumstance as in a marriage.

- Yet beyond all this, there is a way of knowing Jesus Christ that includes all of these yet goes beyond them.

ii. "They tell me he is a refiner, that he cleanses from spots; he has washed me in his precious blood, and to that extent I know him. They tell me that he clothes the naked; he hath covered me with a garment of righteousness, and to that extent I know him. They tell me that he is a breaker, and that he breaks fetters, he has set my soul at liberty, and therefore I know him. They tell me that he is a king and that he reigns over sin; he hath subdued my enemies beneath his feet, and I know him in that character. They tell me he is a shepherd: I know him for I am his sheep. They say he is a door: I have entered in through him, and I know him as a door. They say he is food: my spirit feeds on him as on the bread of heaven, and, therefore, I know him as such." (Spurgeon)

b. **And the power of His resurrection**: Knowing Jesus means knowing this **power**, the new life that is imparted to us *now*, not when we die.

i. "He wants to know in an experiential way the power of Christ's resurrection. That is, he wants to experience the same power that raised Christ from the dead surging through his own being, overcoming sin in his life and producing the Christian graces." (Wuest)

ii. "I do not think, however, that Paul is here thinking so much of the power displayed in the resurrection, as of the power which comes out of it, which may most properly be called, 'the power of his resurrection.' This the apostle desired to apprehend and to know." (Spurgeon)

- The power of His resurrection is an *evidencing power*. It is the evidence and seal that everything Jesus did and said was true.

- The power of His resurrection is a *justifying power*. It is the receipt and proof that the sacrifice of the cross was accepted as payment in full.

- The power of His resurrection is a *life-giving power*. It means that those who are connected with Jesus Christ receive the same resurrection life.

- The power of His resurrection is a *consoling and comforting power*. It promises that our friends and loved ones who are dead in Christ live with Him.

c. **And the fellowship of His sufferings**: Knowing Jesus also means knowing this **fellowship of His sufferings**. It is all part of following Jesus and being *in* Christ. We can say that suffering is part of our heritage as the children of God; we get to be part of the family of suffering: *If children, then heirs - heirs of God and joint heirs with Christ, if indeed we suffer with Him, that we may also be glorified together* (Romans 8:17).

d. **Being conformed to His death**: This reminds us that being **in Christ** also means being "in" His death. These words had particular relevance to Paul who faced possible martyrdom.

e. **If, by any means, I may attain to the resurrection from the dead**: Paul was not morbidly focused on suffering and death in the Christian life. He saw that they were a necessary way to the goal of resurrection life right now and the ultimate resurrection from the dead.

    i. This was a goal that was worth **any means** to Paul. The suffering was worth it, considering the greatness of the goal of **resurrection from the dead**.

    ii. **I may attain**: Paul didn't doubt that he was saved, but he did long mightily for the completion of his salvation through the resurrection of his body. It was something that he had not yet attained and longed for.

    iii. Remember that Paul wrote this having experienced more suffering than we will ever experience, and he wrote it from the custody of Roman soldiers. This wasn't merely theological theory and ideas, but a lived-out connection with God.

4. (12-14) The future of Paul's relationship with Jesus Christ.

Not that I have already attained, or am already perfected; but I press on, that I may lay hold of that for which Christ Jesus has also laid hold of me. Brethren, I do not count myself to have apprehended; but one thing *I do*, forgetting those things which are behind and reaching forward to those things which are ahead, I press toward the goal for the prize of the upward call of God in Christ Jesus.

a. **Not that I have already attained**: Paul wrote from such spiritual maturity and purity that we might expect he believed that he had conquered all spiritual difficulties and saw himself as having arrived at near perfection. Yet he assured us this was not so. There was no perfectionism in Paul.

> i. Sadly, it is common for many Christian leaders to cultivate the attitude that they *have* **already attained**. Without saying the words, they put forth the image of constant triumph that gives the idea that they **have already attained** and are **already perfected**.

> ii. "Brethren, it is a very healthy thing for us who are ministers to read a biography like that of M'Cheyne. Read that through, if you are a minister, and it will burst many of your windbags. You will find yourselves collapse most terribly. Take the life of Brainerd amongst the Indians, or of Baxter in our own land. Think of the holiness of George Herbert, the devoutness of Fletcher, or the zeal of Whitfield. Where do you find yourself after reading their lives? Might you not peep about to find a hiding-place for your insignificance?" (Spurgeon)

> iii. "Just as a little child is a perfect human being, but still is far from perfect in all his development as man, so the true child of God is also perfect in all parts, although not yet perfect in all the stages of his development in faith." (Muller)

> iv. "But while the work of Christ for us is perfect, and it were presumption to think of adding to it, the work of the Holy Spirit in us is not perfect, it is continually carried on from day to day, and will need to be continued throughout the whole of our lives." (Spurgeon)

b. **But I press on**: Because Paul realized that he had not arrived, there was only one option open for him. He had to **press on**. There was no turning back for Him.

> i. When Spain led the world (in the 15th century), her coins reflected her national arrogance and were inscribed *Ne Plus Ultra* which meant "Nothing Further" - meaning that Spain was the ultimate in all the world. After the discovery of the New World, she realized that she was not the end of the world, so Spain changed the inscription on her coinage to *Plus Ultra* meaning "More Beyond." In the same pattern, some Christian lives say, "Nothing Further" and others say "More Beyond."

> ii. This is where child-like faith meets real maturity. A child can't wait to be bigger and always wants to be more mature.

> iii. **But I press on** meant that Paul had put his hand to the plow and refused to look back (Luke 9:62).

c. **That I may lay hold of that for which Christ Jesus has also laid hold of me**: Paul pressed on for what Jesus wanted. His effort was put forth to do God's will, not his own.

> i. When Paul said, "**That I may lay hold**," he used strong language. "The word 'apprehend' is from the same Greek word translated 'attained,' but with a preposition prefixed which means in its local force 'down.' He wants to catch hold of it and pull it down, like a football player who not only wants to catch his man, but wants to pull him down and make him his own." (Wuest)

> ii. Paul began this verse with the idea that Jesus Christ had laid hold of him. This is an important idea; yet sometimes Christians react to that idea by being passive. They suppose, "Jesus got a hold of me; so that is it now. I am a Christian and I am going to heaven." Paul showed a different attitude; he was determined to **lay hold** for that for which Jesus had **laid hold** of him. So one should ask, "Why did Jesus lay hold of Paul?"

> - Jesus **laid hold** of Paul to make him a new man (Romans 6:4) – so Paul would **lay hold** of that and wanted to see the converting work of Jesus completely carried out in himself.

> - Jesus **laid hold** of Paul to conform him into the image of Jesus Christ (Romans 8:29) – so Paul would **lay hold** of that and wanted to see the nature of Jesus within himself.

> - Jesus **laid hold** of Paul to make him a witness (Acts 9:15) – so Paul would **lay hold** of both the experience of Jesus and to testify of that experience.

> - Jesus **laid hold** of Paul to make him an instrument in the conversion of others (Acts 9:15) – so Paul would **lay hold** of the work of bringing others to Jesus.

> - Jesus **laid hold** of Paul to bring him into suffering (Acts 9:16) – so Paul would **lay hold** of even that work of God in his life, wanting to know Jesus in the fellowship of His sufferings.

> - Jesus **laid hold** of Paul that so that the Apostle might attain to the resurrection from the dead (Philippians 3:11) – so Paul would **lay hold** of that heavenly hope.

d. **The prize of the upward call of God in Christ Jesus**: Paul was focused on one thing and would not let **those things which are behind** distract him from it. He pressed on for the **prize**.

i. We often let **those things which are behind** distract us, whether they be good things or bad things. Looking at what is in the past often keeps us from what God has for us in the future.

ii. It is a deception to live either in the past or in the future; God wants us to press on in the present, because the present is where eternity touches us now. Paul knew that a race is won only in the present moment, not in the past or in the future.

e. **I press toward the goal for the prize of the upward call of God in Christ Jesus**: The prize is the **upward call of God**. The **prize** is the **call** itself, not the benefits that come from the call or any other thing. The prize is being able to run the race at all, working with God as a partner to do the work of His kingdom.

i. "It is a *high calling* because it comes from above, from God; the conception of it has emanated from His heart. It is a *high calling* because it is worthy of God. It is a *high calling* because it is so much above the ideals of men.... And then this is a *high calling* because it summons us to where Christ sits at the right hand of God." (Meyer)

ii. Because it is such a glorious call, it is worth **reaching forward** for it. "The Greek word points out the strong exertions made in the *race*; every muscle and nerve is exerted, and he puts forth every particle of his strength in *running*. He was running for life, and running for his life." (Clarke)

f. **The upward call of God in Christ Jesus**: As everything else, this **upward call of God** is only *in* **Christ Jesus**. The legalists might say they followed the **upward call of God**, but they certainly didn't do it **in Christ Jesus**; instead they did it in the efforts of their own flesh.

5. (15-16) Paul exhorts the Philippians to adopt this same attitude.

Therefore let us, as many as are mature, have this mind; and if in anything you think otherwise, God will reveal even this to you. Nevertheless, to *the degree* that we have already attained, let us walk by the same rule, let us be of the same mind.

a. **Therefore let us, as many as are mature, have this mind**: Those who are really **mature** will have this **mind**. If they do not, Paul trusted that God would reveal the necessity of having it.

b. **God will reveal even this to you**: Paul had great trust in the ability of the Lord to deal with His own people. He didn't have the attitude that if *he* failed to convince them, they would then never be convinced.

c. **Nevertheless, to the degree that we have already attained, let us walk by the same rule**: However, Paul would not allow a lack of understanding to excuse anyone from doing what he *did* know to be the Lord's will. What we *don't know* can never excuse us from failing to fulfill what we *do know* to do.

d. **Let us be of the same mind**: Part of doing what we do know is being **of the same mind**. This is a call to unity (a unity of truth, against the potential division brought in by the legalists) that looks back to Philippians 2:1-2.

i. The problems of unity facing the Philippians did not spring from great problems with carnality as was the case with the Corinthians (1 Corinthians 3:1-4). Rather it seemed to be a danger brought on by pressure, both from the outside (Philippians 1:27-30) and from the inside (Philippians 3:2). Paul wanted to make sure that this pressure pushed them *together* instead of driving them *apart*.

C. **Walking the walk.**

1. (17) The good example of walking the walk: Paul and others.

Brethren, join in following my example, and note those who so walk, as you have us for a pattern.

a. **Join in following my example**: We shouldn't think that Paul was being egotistical here. He knew that he was not a sinless or perfect example, yet he was still a *good* example. He could say as he also did in 1 Corinthians 11:1 - *Imitate me, just as I also imitate Christ.*

i. We *need* concrete examples. While it is wrong to put our trust in any man, it is hypocritical for any Christian to say, "Do as I say, *not* as I do."

b. **And note those who so walk**: As well, Paul wasn't so proud to think that he was the *only* one who could be such an example. He told the Philippians to **note those who so walk** in the way he spoke of, and he noted that the Philippians had **us** as a pattern (instead of saying that Paul was the only pattern).

2. (18-19) The bad examples: the **enemies of the cross**.

For many walk, of whom I have told you often, and now tell you even weeping, *that they are* the enemies of the cross of Christ: whose end *is* destruction, whose god *is their* belly, and *whose* glory *is* in their shame— who set their mind on earthly things.

a. **For many walk**: With great sadness, Paul realizes that there are many who **walk** in a manner contrary to what he teaches. He regards these people as **enemies of the cross of Christ**.

i. **The enemies of the cross** were really the opposite of the legalists, who celebrated their supposed liberty in Christ to the indulgence of their flesh.

ii. Paul had to contend with people like this in 1 Corinthians 6:12-20 and Romans 6, who thought that salvation comes without repentance and conversion, and who thought that as long as your soul was saved, it didn't matter what you did with your body.

iii. When we say that men are **enemies of the cross**, we do not mean that they are enemies of a physical representation of the cross. We mean that they are enemies of the Biblical truth of the atonement Jesus made for us on the cross and its ongoing power and effect in our life.

iv. These people were truly **enemies of the *cross* of Christ**, who did not want to follow Jesus by taking up His **cross** of self-denial (Matthew 16:24-26).

b. **And now tell you even weeping**: The work and the end of these **enemies** was that they, in their disregard for God's holiness, gave ammunition to the legalist's accusation that Paul preached a cheap grace that required no commitment of the life. This is what grieved Paul so at their teaching.

i. Spurgeon thought that Paul wept for three reasons. First, on account of the *guilt* of these enemies of the cross of Christ. Second, on account of the *ill effects of their conduct*. Finally, on account of *their doom*.

ii. "I never read that the apostle wept when he was persecuted. Though they ploughed his back with furrows, I do believe that never a tear was seen to gush from his eye while the soldiers scourged him. Though he was cast into prison, we read of his singing, never of his groaning. I do not believe he ever wept on account of any sufferings or dangers to which he himself was exposed for Christ's sake. I call this an extraordinary sorrow, because the man who wept was no soft piece of sentiment, and seldom shed a tear even under grievous trials." (Spurgeon)

iii. "Professors of religion, who get into the church, and yet lead ungodly lives, are the worst enemies that the cross of Christ has. These are the sort of men who bring tears into the minister's eyes; these are they who break his heart; they are the enemies of the cross of Christ." (Spurgeon)

c. **Whose end is destruction**: The word translated **destruction** is the same word used for *perdition* in other places (such as Philippians 1:28). This can refer to either their ultimate damnation or to the present destruction of their lives. Probably their ultimate damnation is more in view.

d. **Whose god is their belly**: This describes the idolatry of these **enemies**. Not that they were necessarily focused on what they eat, but **belly** here has a broader reference to sensual indulgence in general. They live for the pleasures of the body, mind, and soul.

e. **Whose glory is in their shame**: This shows the misplaced priorities of these **enemies**. They gloried about things they should have been ashamed about.

f. **Who set their mind on earthly things**: This describes the focus of their life. It was not to please and worship God, but to get along in *this* world. Their attitude was the same as the rich fool in Luke 12:16-21.

3. (20) Our citizenship and our Lord.

For our citizenship is in heaven, from which we also eagerly wait for the Savior, the Lord Jesus Christ,

a. **For our citizenship is in heaven**: We need to appreciate all this would meant to the Philippians, who greatly valued their Roman citizenship. Just as the Philippians could consider themselves citizens of Rome and were under Roman laws and customs (even though they were in fact far from Rome) so Christians should consider themselves citizens of heaven.

i. One paraphrase of **citizenship is in heaven** reads like this: "We have our home in heaven, and here on earth we are a colony of heaven's citizens." Paul is saying: "Just as the Roman colonists never forgot that they belong to Rome, you must never forget that you are citizens of heaven; and your conduct must match your citizenship." (Barclay)

ii. If we are citizens of heaven, it means that we are resident aliens on earth. Foreigners are distinct in whatever foreign land they go. Christians must be so marked by their heavenly citizenship that they are noticed as different.

- Aliens should seek to do good works in the land they sojourn in.

- Aliens should not seek to interfere in the affairs of the land they sojourn in.

- Aliens have privileges as well as duties; they are not under the same obligations as citizens of the land they sojourn in.

- Aliens are not eligible for the same rewards and recognitions as the citizens of the land that they sojourn in.

- Aliens should not focus on building riches in the land they sojourn in.

iii. We also have a certain character as citizens of heaven.

- As citizens we are under the government of heaven.
- As citizens we share in heaven's honors.
- As citizens we have property rights in heaven.
- As citizens we enjoy the pleasures of heaven.
- As citizens of heaven we love heaven and feel attached there.
- As citizens of heaven we keep in communication with our native home.

iv. "How heartily the Germans sing of the dear old fatherland; but they cannot, with all their Germanic patriotism, they cannot beat the genial glow of the Briton's heart, when he thinks of his fatherland too. The Scotchman, too, wherever he may be, remembers the land of 'brown heath and shaggy wood.' And the Irishman, too, let him be where he will, still thinks the 'Emerald Isle' the first gem of the sea. It is right that the patriot should love his country. Does not our love fervently flame towards heaven?" (Spugeon)

v. There is a significant contrast between the citizens of earth as described in Philippians 3:18-19 and the citizens of heaven as described in Philippians 3:20-21.

b. **From which we also eagerly wait for the Savior**: As Philippians would eagerly await a visit from the emperor in Rome, even more so should Christians eagerly await the coming of their King – Jesus Christ.

i. **Savior** was a title given to the Caesars. In 48 B.C. Julius Caesar was declared to be "the universal savior of mankind." It then became a common title for the ruling Caesar. Paul means something when he applies the title to Jesus in the context of **citizenship**.

c. **The Lord Jesus Christ**: The title **Lord** was also applied to the Roman Caesar. It wasn't long after the time of Paul that Christians were martyred for refusing to call Caesar **Lord**, claiming that Jesus was the only **Lord**.

4. (21) The future work of our Savior: transforming our bodies.

Who will transform our lowly body that it may be conformed to His glorious body, according to the working by which He is able even to subdue all things to Himself.

a. **Who will transform our lowly body that it may be conformed to His glorious body**: Our *Savior* can do and will do something that no Caesar can. When we are resurrected, we will have the same type of body that Jesus Himself had when he was resurrected.

i. Jesus was not merely resuscitated from the dead in the same body. He was resurrected in a new body, patterned after the old yet equipped and fitted for heaven.

b. **According to the working by which He is able even to subdue all things to Himself:** This is possible only because the God we serve is omnipotent. **He is able even to subdue all things to Himself** and accomplish something as amazing as the resurrection of our bodies after the pattern of Jesus' resurrection.

i. Jesus really can **subdue all things**. "There may be sins within your heart that have long resisted control. Do with them as you will, they still defy you... But if you will hand over the conflict to Jesus, He will subdue them; He will bring them under his strong, subjecting hand. Be of good cheer. What you cannot do, He can." (Meyer)

Philippians 4 - Peace and Joy in All Circumstances

A. Instructions to specific saints.

1. (1) A general exhortation: in light of your destiny in Christ, stand fast.

Therefore, my beloved and longed-for brethren, my joy and crown, so stand fast in the Lord, beloved.

> a. **Therefore**: This links together what Paul wrote here with what he wrote before. Because of the promise of resurrection (Philippians 3:21), the Philippians had all the more reason to **stand fast in the Lord**.

> b. **My joy and crown**: Paul used the ancient Greek word for **crown** that described the crown given to an athlete who had won the race. It was a crown of achievement (a *stephanos*); not the crown that was given to a king (a *diadema*). The Philippians, as they **stand fast in the Lord**, were Paul's trophy.

> c. **So stand fast in the Lord, beloved**: We can only **stand fast** when we are **in the Lord**; any other place is not a secure place to stand.

2. (2) Instructions to Euodia and Syntyche.

I implore Euodia and I implore Syntyche to be of the same mind in the Lord.

> a. **Euodia and... Syntyche**: Apparently these two women were the source of some sort of quarrel in the church. Instead of taking sides or trying to solve their problem, Paul simply told them to **be of the same mind in the Lord**.

> b. **To be of the same mind in the Lord**: Whatever the dispute was about, **Euodia** and **Syntyche** had forgotten that they have a greater common ground in Jesus Christ. They forgot that everything else was less important than that common ground.

3. (3) Instructions to the **true companion**.

And I urge you also, true companion, help these women who labored with me in the gospel, with Clement also, and the rest of my fellow workers, whose names *are* in the Book of Life.

a. **I urge you also, true companion**: Whoever this was, Paul instructed them to **help these women who labored with me in the gospel**. The **true companion** was supposed to **help** these women to reconcile and come to one mind in the Lord.

i. **These women who labored with me in the gospel** is a telling phrase. These two women, Euodia and Syntyche, were faithful workers with Paul in the work of the gospel. Yet, they had a falling out with each other. Paul knew that this unfortunate dispute needed to be cleared up.

b. **With Clement also**: There was a notable **Clement** in the early church who was the leader of the church in Rome and wrote two preserved letters to the church in Corinth. Yet we don't know if this is the same Clement. It was a common name in the Roman world.

i. We can contrast the brief mention of Euodia and Syntyche with the brief mention of Clement. If you had to have your whole life summed up in one sentence, would you like it to be summed up like Clement or like Euodia and Syntyche?

c. **And the rest of my fellow workers, whose names are in the Book of Life**: There were others in Philippi who also helped Paul. They had the greatest honor in the world: to have their names in **the Book of Life** (Revelation 20:15).

B. More instruction on walking the walk.

1. (4) Paul repeats a major theme of the letter.

Rejoice in the Lord always. Again I will say, rejoice!

a. **Rejoice**: Despite the circumstance from which it was written, *joy* is all over the letter to the Philippians. Examples of this are in Philippians 1:4, 1:18, 1:25, 2:2, 2:16, 2:17, 2:18, 2:28, 3:1, 3:3, and 4:1.

i. "I am glad that we do not know what the quarrel was about; I am usually thankful for ignorance on such subjects; - but as a cure for disagreements, the apostle says, 'Rejoice in the Lord always.' People who are very happy, especially those who are very happy in the Lord, are not apt either to give offense or to take offense. Their minds are so sweetly occupied with higher things, that they are not easily distracted by the little troubles which naturally arise among such imperfect creatures as we are. Joy in the Lord is the cure for all discord." (Spurgeon)

b. **Rejoice in the Lord always**: Again, Paul's joy wasn't based in a sunny optimism or positive mental attitude as much as it was the confidence that God was in control. It really was a joy **in the Lord**.

i. "What a gracious God we serve, who makes delight to be a duty, and who commands us to rejoice! Should we not at once be obedient to such a command as this? It is intended that we should be happy." (Spurgeon)

2. (5) Show a gentle disposition to all men.

Let your gentleness be known to all men. The Lord *is* at hand.

a. **Let your gentleness be known**: Paul used an interesting ancient Greek word (*epieikeia*) that is translated **gentleness** here. Other translations of the Bible translate *epieikeia* as patience, softness, the patient mind, modesty, forbearance, the forbearing spirit, or magnanimity.

i. "The word *epieikes* is of very extensive signification; it means the same as *epieikeia*, mildness, patience, yieldingness, gentleness, clemency, *moderation*, unwillingness to litigate or contend; but *moderation* is expressive enough as a general term." (Clarke)

ii. A good example of this quality is when Jesus showed **gentleness** with the woman who was taken in adultery in a set-up and brought to Jesus. He knew how to show a holy **gentleness** to her.

iii. This word describes the heart of a person who will let the Lord fight his battles. He knows that *vengeance is Mine, says the Lord* (Romans 12:19). It describes a person who is really free to let go of His anxieties and all the things that cause him stress, because he knows that the Lord will take up his cause.

b. **Be known to all men**: The sphere is broad. We show this gentleness to **all men**, not just to whom we please.

c. **The Lord is at hand**: When we live with the awareness of Jesus' soon return, it makes it all the more easy to *rejoice in the Lord* and to show **gentleness** to all men. We know that Jesus will settle every wrong at His return, and we can trust Him to make things right in our falling-apart world.

3. (6) A living prayer life.

Be anxious for nothing, but in everything by prayer and supplication, with thanksgiving, let your requests be made known to God;

a. **Be anxious for nothing**: This is a command, not an option. Undue care is an intrusion into an arena that belongs to God alone. It makes us the father of the household instead of being a child.

b. **But in everything by prayer and supplication**: Paul wrote that **everything** is the proper subject of prayer. There are not some areas of our lives that are of no concern to God.

c. **Prayer and supplication**: These two aspects of prayer are similar, but distinct. **Prayer** is a broader word that can mean all of our communication with God, but **supplication** directly asks God to do something.

    i. Many of our prayers go unanswered because we do not *ask* God for anything. Here God invites us simply to **let your requests be made known**. He wants to know.

d. **Be made known**: God already knows our requests before we pray them; yet He will often *wait* for our participation through prayer before granting that which we request.

e. **With thanksgiving**: This guards against a whining, complaining spirit before God when we let our requests be made known. We really can be anxious for nothing, pray about everything, and be thankful for anything.

4. (7) The promise of peace.

And the peace of God, which surpasses all understanding, will guard your hearts and minds through Christ Jesus.

a. **And the peace of God**: The Bible describes three great aspects of **peace** that relate to God.

- *Peace from God:* Paul continually used this as an introduction to his letters; it reminds us that our peace comes to us as a gift from God.

- *Peace with God:* This describes a relationship that we enter into with God through the finished work of Jesus Christ.

- **The peace of God**: This is the peace spoken of in Philippians 4:7. It is beyond "all mind"; that is, beyond our power of thinking.

    i. "What is God's peace? The unruffled serenity of the infinitely-happy God, the eternal composure of the absolutely well-contented God." (Spurgeon)

b. **Which surpasses all understanding**: It isn't that it is senseless and therefore impossible to understand, but that it is beyond our ability to understand and to explain - therefore it must be *experienced*.

    i. This peace doesn't just surpass the understanding of the worldly man; it surpasses **all understanding**. Even the godly man can not comprehend this peace.

c. **Guard your hearts and minds**: The word **guard** speaks of a military action. This is something that the peace of God does for us; it is a peace that is on **guard** over our heart and mind.

i. "Shall keep them as in a strong place or a castle." (Clarke)

ii. When people seem to "lose" their heart or mind, it often is connected to an absence of the peace of God in their life. The peace of God then does not act as a **guard** for their **hearts and minds**.

5. (8) The right place to put our minds.

Finally, brethren, whatever things are true, whatever things *are* noble, whatever things *are* just, whatever things *are* pure, whatever things *are* lovely, whatever things *are* of good report, if *there is* any virtue and if *there is* anything praiseworthy—meditate on these things.

a. **Whatever things are true**: Paul's list of things on which we should meditate translates well from the Greek to the English; there is no great need for elaboration upon each item.

b. **Noble... just... pure... lovely... good report... virtue... praiseworthy**: These, Paul would say, are the fruit and the food of the mind that is guarded by the peace of God. When we put these good things into our mind, they *stay* in our mind and then come forth from us.

c. **Meditate on these things**: Much of the Christian life comes down to the *mind*. Romans 12:2 speaks of the essential place of being *transformed by the renewing of your mind* and 2 Corinthians 10:5 speaks of the importance of *casting down arguments and every high thing that exalts itself against the knowledge of God, bringing every thought into captivity to the obedience of Christ*. What we choose to **meditate on** matters.

i. What Paul describes here is a practical way to bring *every thought into captivity to the obedience of Christ*.

6. (9) A return to the idea of following Paul's example.

The things which you learned and received and heard and saw in me, these do, and the God of peace will be with you.

a. **The things which you learned and received and heard and saw in me, these do**: Paul had the integrity to present himself as an example of all these things to the Philippians. He really could say, "Follow me as I follow Jesus."

b. **And the God of peace will be with you**: If the Philippians did as Paul had instructed, not only would they have had the peace *of* God, but the **God of peace** would have also been with them.

C. Paul comments on the giving of the Philippians.

1. (10-14) Paul's perspective on the gift from the Philippians.

But I rejoiced in the Lord greatly that now at last your care for me has flourished again; though you surely did care, but you lacked opportunity. Not that I speak in regard to need, for I have learned in whatever state I am, to be content: I know how to be abased, and I know how to abound. Everywhere and in all things I have learned both to be full and to be hungry, both to abound and to suffer need. I can do all things through Christ who strengthens me. Nevertheless you have done well that you shared in my distress.

a. **Your care for me has flourished again**: This refers to the financial support brought by Epaphroditus (Philippians 2:25). Paul didn't want to imply that the Philippians didn't care before, only that before they **lacked opportunity**. When they had the opportunity, then their **care** for Paul **flourished again**.

b. **Not that I speak in regard to need**: Paul reminded the Philippians that his thankfulness for the Philippians' giving wasn't *because* he was needy (though he was in fact in need), but because it was good for *them* to be givers.

c. **I have learned in whatever state I am, to be content**: This was *how* Paul could say that his thankfulness was not based upon his own need. Even though Paul was in need, he was content where he was at – even in his Roman imprisonment.

i. **I have learned**: Paul had to *learn* contentment; it isn't natural to mankind.

ii. **I know how to be abased, and I know how to abound**: Paul reminds us that his contentment was not only theoretical. He actually *lived* this. Paul *had* been financially well-off; he *had* been financially needy.

iii. Paul knew **how to be abased**. "See here the state to which God permitted his chief apostle to be reduced! And see how powerfully the grace of Christ supported him under the whole! How few of those who are called Christian ministers or Christian men have learned this important lesson! When want or affliction comes, their complaints are loud and frequent; and they are soon at the end of their patience." (Clarke)

iv. Paul also knew **how to abound**. "There are a great many men that know a little how to be abased, that do not know at all how to abound. When they are put down into the pit with Joseph, they look up and see the starry promise, and they hope for an escape. But when they are put on the top of a pinnacle, their heads grow dizzy, and they are ready to fall." (Spurgeon)

d. **I can do all things through Christ who strengthens me**: This refers to Paul's ability to be content in all things. To achieve this contentment, he needed the strength of Jesus Christ.

i. Unfortunately, many people take this verse out of context and use it to reinforce a "triumphalist" or "super-Christian" mentality, instead of seeing that the strength of Jesus in Paul's life was evident in his ability **to be content** when he did **suffer need**.

ii. We must always also put this precious statement of faith in connection with John 15:5: *for without Me you can do nothing*. With Jesus we can do all things, without Him we can't do anything.

e. **Nevertheless you have done well that you shared in my distress**: In speaking about his ability to be content, Paul did not want to give the impression that the Philippians had somehow done something wrong in supporting Paul. But there was a real sense in which the giving of the Philippians was better *for them* than it was for Paul (**you have done well**). Godly giving actually does more good for the giver than for the one who receives.

2. (15-18) Thanks for the past and present giving of the Philippians.

Now you Philippians know also that in the beginning of the gospel, when I departed from Macedonia, no church shared with me concerning giving and receiving but you only. For even in Thessalonica you sent *aid* once and again for my necessities. Not that I seek the gift, but I seek the fruit that abounds to your account. Indeed I have all and abound. I am full, having received from Epaphroditus the things *sent* from you, a sweet-smelling aroma, an acceptable sacrifice, well pleasing to God.

a. **The beginning of the gospel**: This refers to Paul's pioneering missionary efforts in Europe, recorded in Acts 16 and following.

b. **No church shared with me concerning giving and receiving but you only**: The Philippians were the only ones to support Paul during this particular period. Paul especially remembered how they supported him when he was in Thessalonica.

i. "Probably the gift does not come to very much, if estimated in Roman coin; but he makes a great deal of it, and sits down to write a letter of thanks abounding in rich expressions like these." (Spurgeon)

ii. "While labouring to plant the church there, he was supported partly by working with his hands, 1 Thessalonians 2:9; 2 Thessalonians 3:7-9; and partly by the contributions sent him from Philippi. Even the Thessalonians had contributed little to his maintenance: this is not spoken to their credit." (Clarke)

c. **Not that I seek the gift, but I seek the fruit that abounds to your account**: Paul wasn't so much interested in the **gift** on his own behalf, but in the **fruit that abounds to your account**. Their giving increased the fruit in their **account** before God.

i. "It is not the actual gift put into Paul's hands which has brought him joy, but the giving and the meaning of that giving. It is the truest index to the abiding reality of his work." (Expositors)

ii. This reflects one of the most important principles regarding giving in the Scriptures: that we are never the poorer for having given. God will never be our debtor, and we can never out-give God.

d. **A sweet-smelling aroma, an acceptable sacrifice, well pleasing to God**: Paul described the gift of the Philippians in terms that remind us of sacrifices in the Old Testament (Genesis 8:21, Exodus 29:18, 29:25, and 29:41). Our giving to God's work is similar to Old Testament sacrifices, which also cost the person bringing the sacrifice a lot. Bulls and rams did not come cheaply in that day.

i. Ephesians 5:2 uses the same terminology in reference to Jesus' sacrifice for us; our sacrifices are likewise pleasing to God as **a sweet-smelling aroma**.

ii. In 2 Corinthians 8:1-5, Paul boasted about the Philippians as an example of the right kind of giving. He describes how they gave *willingly*, out of their own *need*, and they gave after *first having given themselves* to the Lord.

3. (19) Paul declares a promise to the Philippians regarding their own financial needs.

And my God shall supply all your need according to His riches in glory by Christ Jesus.

a. **My God shall supply all your need**: We shouldn't think that the Philippians were wealthy benefactors of Paul who could easily spare the money. As Paul described them in 2 Corinthians 8, it is plain that their giving was sacrificial. This promise *meant* something to them!

i. "He says to them, 'You have helped me; but my God shall supply you. You have helped me in one of my needs-my need of clothing and of food: I have other needs in which you could not help me; but my God shall supply all your need. You have helped me, some of you, out of your deep poverty, taking from your scanty store; but my God shall supply all your need out of his riches in glory.'" (Spurgeon)

b. **Shall supply all your need**: The promise is to supply *all* your need; but it is **all your *need*** (not a promise to go beyond needs) In this, the promise is both broad and yet restricted.

c. **According to His riches in glory by Christ Jesus**: This is a staggering *measure* of giving. Since there is no lack in God's **riches in glory**, we should anticipate that there would be no lack in God's supply.

i. "The rewarding will not be merely from His wealth, but also in a manner that befits His wealth - on a scale worthy of His wealth." (Martin)

ii. Spurgeon thought that this verse was a great illustration of that wonderful miracle in 2 Kings 4:1-7, where Elisha told the widow to gather empty vessels, set them out, and pour forth the oil from the one small vessel of oil she had into the empty vessels. She filled and filled and miraculously filled until every empty vessel was full.

- *All our need* is like the empty vessels.
- *God* is the one who fills the empty vessels.
- *According to His riches in glory* describes the style in which God fills the empty vessels – the oil keeps flowing until every available vessel is filled.
- *By Christ Jesus* describes the how God meets our needs – our empty vessels are filled by Jesus in all His glory.

d. **All your need**: We also notice that this promise was made to the Philippians – those who had surrendered their finances and material possessions to God's service, and who knew how to give with the right kind of heart.

i. This promise simply expresses what Jesus said in Luke 6:38: *Give, and it will be given to you: good measure, pressed down, shaken together, and running over will be put into your bosom. For with the same measure that you use, it will be measured back to you.*

D. Conclusion to the letter.

1. (20) A brief doxology.

Now to our God and Father *be* glory forever and ever. Amen.

a. **Be glory forever and ever**: It is wrong to think of this as an unthinking comment made by Paul in the way that we throw off comments like "glory to God" or "praise the Lord" in our Christian culture. Paul genuinely wanted God to be glorified and was willing to be used in whatever way God saw fit to glorify Himself (Philippians 1:20).

b. **Amen**: This was a word borrowed from Hebrew meaning, "So be it." It is an expression of confident and joyful affirmation.

2. (21-22) Mutual greetings expressed.

Greet every saint in Christ Jesus. The brethren who are with me greet you. All the saints greet you, but especially those who are of Caesar's household.

a. **Greet every saint**: Paul did not here give specific greetings to individuals as he did in other letters. Rather, he greeted **every saint** in Christ Jesus. This also is another example of the fact that the title **saint** applies to all Christians, not just to an elite few.

b. **All the saints greet you, but especially those who are of Caesar's household**: This special greeting is evidence that Paul was still used by God during his Roman imprisonment, when the gospel extended even into the household of Caesar.

i. **Those who are of Caesar's household**: "By this he designates the functionaries and servants and slaves of the Emperor's household, with whom Paul, as a prisoner for several years, undoubtedly came in contact on several occasions." (Muller)

ii. "Nero was at this time emperor of Rome: a more worthless, cruel, and diabolic wretch never disgraced the name or form of man; yet in *his family* there were Christians: but whether this relates to the members of the *imperial family*, or to *guards*, or *courtiers*, or to *servants*, we cannot tell." (Clarke)

3. (23) Final words.

The grace of our Lord Jesus Christ be with you all. Amen.

a. **The grace of our Lord Jesus Christ be with you all**: Paul did not say this to simply fill up space at the end of his letter. To him, the Christian life begins and ends with the **grace of our Lord Jesus Christ**, so it was appropriate that his letters began and ended with **grace** also.

b. **Amen**: This was a fitting word of affirmation. Paul knew that what he wrote to the Philippians was worthy to be agreed with, so he added the final word of agreement - **Amen**.

Colossians 1 - The Greatness of Jesus Christ

A. Greeting and giving of thanks.

1. (1-2) Paul greets the Christians in Colosse.

Paul, an apostle of Jesus Christ by the will of God, and Timothy our brother, to the saints and faithful brethren in Christ *who are* in Colosse: Grace to you and peace from God our Father and the Lord Jesus Christ.

a. **Paul**: According to the custom of writing letters in that day, the author's name is given first. Therefore the author was **Paul**; he wrote the letter while in Roman custody (Colossians 4:3, 4:10, and 4:18), probably from Rome and around A.D. 63.

i. Paul probably wrote the letter because of the visit of Epaphras from Colosse (Colossians 1:7). It is likely that Paul himself had never visited the city (Colossians 2:1).

b. **An apostle of Jesus Christ by the will of God**: Paul was qualified to write this letter of instruction to the Colossians, though he had never met them personally, because he was **an apostle**.

i. "The literal meaning of *apostolos* is 'one sent'; but at its deepest level it denotes an authorized spokesman for God, one commissioned and empowered to act as his representative." (Vaughan)

ii. **And Timothy our brother**: Timothy was an honored companion of Paul, but he was not an **apostle**. "Though Timothy is here joined in the salutation, yet he has never been understood as having any part in composing this epistle. He has been considered as the amanuensis or scribe of the apostle." (Clarke)

c. **To the saints and faithful brethren**: When Paul addressed the **saints**, he did not separate some Christians from others in the Colossian church. Every true Christian is a saint. However, Paul may make a distinction with the phrase **faithful brethren**. He may refer to those who haven't embraced the false teaching that concerned Paul so much in this letter.

d. **Who are in Colosse**: The city of Colosse was probably the smallest and least important city that Paul ever wrote to. It might surprise us that Paul would turn his attention to the Christians in **Colosse** at a time when he had so many other concerns. Yet he apparently thought the situation in Colosse was important enough for apostolic attention.

i. Paul wrote because there were problems among the Christians in Colosse, but the doctrinal problem – sometimes described as "The Colossian Heresy" – is difficult to precisely describe. It probably was a corruption of Christianity with elements of mystical and legalistic Judaism perhaps combined with early Gnosticism.

ii. The first century religious environment was much like our own. It was a time of religious mixing, with people borrowing a little from this religion and a little from that religion. The only difference was that in the first century, one joined a *group* who did the borrowing. In our modern culture one does the borrowing *one's self.*

iii. Whatever the problem was precisely, Paul dwelt on the solution: *a better understanding of Jesus*. Knowing the *real* Jesus helps us to stay away from the counterfeit, no matter how it comes packaged.

e. **In Colosse**: The city of **Colosse** is not even mentioned in the Book of Acts. All our Biblical information about the church there comes from this letter and a few allusions in the letter to Philemon.

i. From these sources we learn that Epaphras was responsible for bringing the gospel to the Colossians (Colossians 1:6-7). He was a native of the city (Colossians 4:12), and also got the message out to neighboring towns in the Lycus Valley like Hierapolis and Laodicea (Colossians 4:13).

ii. Perhaps Epaphras heard the gospel himself when Paul was in Ephesus. As Paul taught in the lecture hall of Tyrannus, *all the residents of Asia heard the word of the Lord* (Acts 19:10). It would not be surprising if some people from Colosse heard the gospel at that time.

iii. Historically, **Colosse** was a prosperous city, and famous (along with other cities in its region) for its fabric dyes. Yet by Paul's time the glory it had as a city was on the decline.

iv. Adam Clarke adds an interesting comment: "That this city perished by an earthquake, a short time after the date of this epistle, we have the testimony of Eusebius." Tacitus also mentioned this earthquake, which happened around A.D. 60.

f. **Grace to you and peace from God the Father and our Lord Jesus Christ**: Paul's greeting was familiar but heartfelt. "Grace is God's unconditioned goodwill toward men and women which is decisively expressed in the saving work of Christ." (Bruce)

> i. This letter – full of love and concern, written to a church Paul had neither planted nor visited – shows the power of Christian love. Paul didn't need to see or meet or directly know these Christians in order to love them and be concerned for them.

2. (3) Paul's habit of prayer for the Colossians.

We give thanks to the God and Father of our Lord Jesus Christ, praying always for you,

> a. **Praying always for you**: Though he had never met most of them, the Christians of Colosse were on Paul's prayer list. He prayed for them not only often, but **always**.
>
> b. **We give thanks**: When Paul did pray for the Colossians, he did it full of gratitude. Perhaps those who pray the most end up having the most reasons to thank God.

3. (4-8) Why Paul was thankful.

Since we heard of your faith in Christ Jesus and of your love for all the saints; because of the hope which is laid up for you in heaven, of which you heard before in the word of the truth of the gospel, which has come to you, as *it has* also in all the world, and is bringing forth fruit, as *it is* also among you since the day you heard and knew the grace of God in truth; as you also learned from Epaphras, our dear fellow servant, who is a faithful minister of Christ on your behalf, who also declared to us your love in the Spirit.

> a. **Since we heard**: Paul was thankful for their **faith in Christ Jesus** and their **love for all the saints**. Genuine **faith** in Jesus will always have a true **love** for God's people as a companion.
>
> b. **Because of the hope**: Paul was thankful for the **hope** laid up for them in heaven. He was thankful when he considered the destiny of the Colossian Christians.
>
> > i. We notice the familiar triad of **faith**, **hope**, and **love**. These were not merely theological ideas to Paul; they dominated his thinking as a Christian.
>
> c. **Which you heard before in the word of the truth**: Paul was thankful that their eternal destiny was affected by the **truth of the gospel**, brought by Epaphras (**as you also learned from Epaphras**).
>
> > i. Epaphras is described as **a faithful minister of Christ on your behalf**. This doesn't mean that Epaphras was *superior* to the other

Christians in Colosse. The word **minister** does not mean "superior"; it means "one who serves."

d. **And is bringing forth fruit**: Paul was thankful that the gospel was **bringing forth fruit** over **all the world**, even while Paul was in a Roman prison.

> i. The phrase "**in all the world**" was "A legitimate hyperbole, for the gospel was spreading all over the Roman Empire." (Robertson)

> ii. "The doctrine of the Gospel is represented as a *traveller*, whose object it is to visit the whole habitable earth... So rapid is this *traveller* in his course, that he had already gone nearly through the whole of the countries under the Roman dominion, and will travel on until he has proclaimed his message to every people, and kindred, and nation, and tongue." (Clarke)

B. How Paul prayed for the Colossian Christians.

1. (9-11) Paul petitions God on behalf of the Colossians.

For this reason we also, since the day we heard it, do not cease to pray for you, and to ask that you may be filled with the knowledge of His will in all wisdom and spiritual understanding; that you may walk worthy of the Lord, fully pleasing *Him*, being fruitful in every good work and increasing in the knowledge of God; strengthened with all might, according to His glorious power, for all patience and longsuffering with joy;

a. **To ask that you may be filled with the knowledge of His will**: First, Paul prayed that they would have a **knowledge of His will**, informed by a true **spiritual understanding**. To *know God* and *what He requires of us* is our first responsibility.

> i. "If you read this epistle through, you will observe that Paul frequently alludes to knowledge and wisdom. To the point in which be judged the church to be deficient he turned his prayerful attention. He would not have them ignorant. He knew that spiritual ignorance is the constant source of error, instability, and sorrow; and therefore he desired that they might be soundly taught in the things of God." (Spurgeon)

b. **That you may walk worthy of the Lord, fully pleasing Him**: Second, Paul prayed that they would live according to the same knowledge they received, living out a **walk worthy of the Lord**.

> i. This is a familiar pattern, repeated over and over again in the New Testament. Our walk is based on our knowledge of God and our understanding of His will.

c. **Being fruitful in every good work** and **increasing in the knowledge of God**. This is how we can be **fully pleasing** to God and how we can have a **worthy** walk.

> i. This is an echo of Jesus' thought in John 15:7-8: *If you abide in Me, and My words abide in you, you will ask what you desire and it shall be done for you. By this My Father is glorified, that you bear much fruit; so you will be My disciples.*

> ii. "'Fruitful in every good work.' Here is room and range enough – in 'every good work.' Have you the ability to preach the gospel? Preach it! Does a little child need comforting? Comfort it! Can you stand up and vindicate a glorious truth before thousands? Do it! Does a poor saint need a bit of dinner from your table? Send it to her. Let works of obedience, testimony, zeal, charity, piety, and philanthropy all be found in your life. Do not select big things as your special line, but glorify the Lord also in the littles – 'fruitful in every good work.'" (Spurgeon)

d. **Strengthened with all might**: As we **walk worthy of the Lord**, His strength is there to help us meet all of life's challenges, and to endure and overcome problems with circumstances (**patience**) and people (**longsuffering**) with joy.

2. (12-14) Paul's specific thanks to the Father.

Giving thanks to the Father who has qualified us to be partakers of the inheritance of the saints in the light. He has delivered us from the power of darkness and conveyed *us* into the kingdom of the Son of His love, in whom we have redemption through His blood, the forgiveness of sins.

a. **Giving thanks to the Father who has qualified us**: In the divine administration, the Father is mentioned in connection with the broad sweep of His plan of redemption. He is the Person of the Trinity who *initiates* the plan of the ages.

b. **To be partakers of the inheritance of the saints**: It is the Father who qualifies us, not our own works. We gain this as an **inheritance**, instead of earning it as a wage.

c. **He has delivered us from the power of darkness**: Christians have been **delivered** from Satan's domain. The word has the idea of a rescue by a sovereign power.

> i. Another place where this same phrase for **power of darkness** is used is in Luke 22:53, where Jesus spoke of the darkness surrounding His arrest and passion in the same terms. "These words refer to the sinister

forces marshaled against him for decisive combat in the spiritual realm." (Bruce)

ii. The **power of darkness** may be seen in its effects, and for those who have been **delivered... from the power of darkness** these effects should be less and less evident in the life.

- The power of darkness lulls us to sleep.
- The power of darkness is skilled at concealment.
- The power of darkness afflicts and depresses man.
- The power of darkness can fascinate us.
- The power of darkness emboldens some men.

iii. "Beloved, we still are tempted by Satan, but we are not under his power; we have to fight with him, but we are not his slaves. He is not our king; he has no rights over us; we do not obey him; we will not listen to his temptations." (Spurgeon)

d. **And conveyed us into the kingdom of the Son of His love**: According to Barclay, the word we translate **conveyed** had a special significance in the ancient world. When one empire conquered another, the custom was to take the population of the defeated empire and transfer it completely to the conqueror's land. It is in this sense that Paul says we have been **conveyed** into God's kingdom. Everything we have and everything we are now belongs to Him.

i. **The Son of His love** is a Hebraic way of saying "God's dear Son."

e. **In whom we have redemption through His blood**: Redemption has the idea of release by a legal ransom. The price for our release was paid by the blood of Jesus.

i. This is one reason why pleading the blood of Jesus – in the right sense, not in a magical or superstitious sense – has such great significance in spiritual warfare. It shows the "receipt" of our lawful purchase as redeemed people.

ii. One of the great sticky questions of theology is *to whom was the price paid?* Some say it was to *God* that the ransom price was paid, but we were prisoners of *Satan's* kingdom. Others say it was to *Satan* that the ransom price was paid, but what does God owe to Satan? This question probably simply extends the metaphor too far.

f. **The forgiveness of sins**: The word translated **forgiveness** is the ancient Greek word *aphesis*, most literally rendered "a sending away." Our sin and guilt is *sent away* because of what Jesus did on the cross for us.

i. "It thus speaks of the removal of our sins from us, so that they are no longer barriers that separate us from God." (Vaughan)

3. (15-20) Paul's meditation on the person and work of Jesus.

He is the image of the invisible God, the firstborn over all creation. For by Him all things were created that are in heaven and that are on earth, visible and invisible, whether thrones or dominions or principalities or powers. All things were created through Him and for Him. And He is before all things, and in Him all things consist. And He is the head of the body, the church, who is the beginning, the firstborn from the dead, that in all things He may have the preeminence. For it pleased *the Father that* in Him all the fullness should dwell, and by Him to reconcile all things to Himself, by Him, whether things on earth or things in heaven, having made peace through the blood of His cross.

a. **He is**: Paul started out thanking the Father for His plan of redemption (Colossians 1:12). He couldn't do that without also thinking of the Son, who is the great Redeemer.

i. Most scholars think that Colossians 1:15-20 came from a poem or a hymn in the early Church that described what Christians believed about Jesus. This is entirely possible, but can't be proven one way or another.

b. **He is the image of the invisible God**: The word translated **image** (the ancient Greek word *eikon*) expressed two ideas.

• *Likeness*, as in the image on a coin or the reflection in a mirror.

• *Manifestation*, with the sense that God is fully revealed in Jesus.

i. If Paul meant that Jesus was merely similar to the Father, he would have used the ancient Greek word *homoioma*, which speaks merely of similar appearance. The stronger word used here proves that Paul knew that Jesus is God just as God the Father is God. It means that "Jesus is the very stamp of God the Father." (Robertson)

ii. "God is invisible, which does not merely mean that He cannot be seen by our bodily eye, but that He is unknowable. In the exalted Christ the unknowable God becomes known." (Peake)

iii. According to Barclay, the ancient Jewish philosopher Philo equated the *eikon* of God with the *Logos*. Paul used this important and meaningful word with great purpose.

c. **The firstborn over all creation**: **Firstborn** (the ancient Greek word *prototokos*) can describe either priority in time or supremacy in rank. As Paul used it here, he probably had both ideas in mind, with Jesus being before all created things and Jesus being of a supremely different order than all created things.

i. **Firstborn** is also used of Jesus in Colossians 1:18, Romans 8:29, Hebrews 1:6, and Revelation 1:5.

ii. In no way does the title **firstborn** indicate that Jesus is less than God. In fact, the ancient Rabbis called Yawhew Himself "Firstborn of the World" (Rabbi Bechai, cited in Lightfoot). Ancient rabbis used **firstborn** as a Messianic title: "God said, As I made Jacob a first-born (Exodus 4:22), so also will I make king Messiah a first-born (Psalm 89:27)." (R. Nathan in *Shemoth Rabba*, cited in Lightfoot)

iii. "The use of this word does not show what Arius argued: that Paul regarded Christ as a creature like 'all creation'... It is rather the comparative (superlative) force of *protos* that is used." (Robertson)

iv. Bishop Lightfoot, a noted Greek scholar, on the use of both *eikon* (**image**) and *prototokos* (**firstborn**): "As the Person of Christ was the Divine response alike to the philosophical questionings of the Alexandrian Jew and to the patriotic hopes of the Palestinian, these two currents of thought meet in the term *prototokos* as applied to our Lord, who is both the true Logos and the true Messiah." (Lightfoot)

v. "*Prototokos* in its primary sense expresses temporal priority, and then, on account of the privileges of the firstborn, it gains the further sense of dominion... Whether the word retains anything of its original meaning here is doubtful." (Peake)

d. **For by Him all things were created**: There is no doubt that Jesus is the author of *all* creation. He Himself is not a created being. When we behold the wonder and the glory of the world Jesus **created**, we worship and honor Him all the more.

i. Comets have vapor trails up to 10,000 miles long. If you could capture all that vapor, and put it in a bottle, the amount of vapor actually present in the bottle would take up less than 1 cubic inch of space.

ii. Saturn's rings are 500,000 miles in circumference, but only about a foot thick.

iii. If the sun were the size of a beachball and put on top of the Empire State Building, the nearest group of stars would be as far away as Australia is to the Empire State Building.

iv. The earth travels around the sun about eight times the speed of a bullet fired from a gun.

v. There are more insects in one square mile of rural land than there are human beings on the entire earth.

vi. A single human chromosome contains twenty billion bits of information. How much information is that? If written in ordinary books, in ordinary language, it would take about four thousand volumes.

vii. According to Greek scholar A.T. Robertson, **all things were created** has the idea of "stand created" or "remain created." Robertson adds: "The permanence of the universe rests, then, on Christ far more than on gravity. It is a Christ-centric universe."

e. **Whether thrones or dominions or principalities or powers**: As will be demonstrated in the rest of the letter, the Colossian Heresy seemed taken with an elaborate angelology, which effectively placed angels as mediators between God and man. Paul emphasized that whatever ranks of spirit beings there may be, Jesus created them all and they all ultimately answer to Him.

f. **He is before all things... who is the beginning**: Centuries after Paul, a dangerous (yet popular) teacher named Arius claimed that Jesus was not truly God and that there was a time when He did not exist. Paul rightly understood and insisted that Jesus **is before all things** and is Himself **the beginning**.

i. "As all creation necessarily exists in *time*, and had a *commencement*, and there was an infinite duration in which it *did not exist*, whatever was *before* or *prior* to that must be *no part of creation*; and the Being who existed prior to creation, *and before all things*-all existence of every kind, must be the unoriginated and eternal God: but Paul says, *Jesus Christ was before all things*; ergo, the apostle conceived Jesus Christ to be truly, and essentially God." (Clarke)

g. **In Him all things consist**: The idea that Jesus is both the unifying principle and the personal sustainer of all creation.

i. "Hence, God, as the *Preserver*, is as necessary to the continuance of all things, as God the *Creator* was to their original production. But this *preserving* or *continuing* power is here ascribed to *Christ*." (Clarke)

h. **Head of the body, the church**: This describes Jesus' relationship to the church. Here, **head** probably refers to Jesus' role as **source** of the church, even as we refer to the **head** of a river.

i. **That in all things He may have the preeminence**: This is a fitting summary of the verses found in Colossians 1:15-18.

i. Adam Clarke on Colossians 1:16-17: "Now, allowing St. Paul to have understood the terms which he used, he must have considered Jesus Christ as being truly and properly *God*... Unless there be some secret way of understanding the 16th and 17th verses, which God has nowhere revealed, taken in their sober and rational sense and meaning they must forever settle this very important point."

j. **Fullness**: This translates the ancient Greek word *pleroma*, and was really just another way to say that Jesus is truly God.

i. The word **fullness** was "a recognized technical term in theology, denoting the totality of the Divine powers and attributes." (Lightfoot, cited in Robertson)

ii. According to Vincent, *pleroma* was used by the Gnostic teachers in a technical sense, to express the sum-total of divine powers and attributes "Christ may have been ranked with these inferior images of the divine by the Colossian teachers. Hence the significance of the assertion that the *totality* of the divine dwells in Him." (Vincent)

iii. "The Gnostics distributed the divine powers among various aeons. Paul gathers them all up in Christ, a full and flat statement of the deity of Christ." (Robertson)

k. **For it pleased the Father that in Him all the fullness should dwell**: The ancient Greek word for **dwell** is here used in the sense of a *permanent dwelling*. There is an entirely different word used for the sense of a *temporary* dwelling place. Paul wanted to emphasize the idea that Jesus was not *temporarily* God, but is *permanently* God.

i. "Two mighty words; *'fullness'* a substantial, comprehensive, expressive word in itself, and 'all,' a great little word including everything. When combined in the expression, *'all fullness,'* we have before us a superlative wealth of meaning." (Spurgeon)

ii. Once it pleased the Father to bruise Him (Isaiah 53:10); now it pleases the Father that in Him all the fullness of God should dwell.

iii. "Thus the phrase *in Him should all the fullness dwell* gathers into a grand climax the previous statements - *image of God, first-born of all creation, Creator, the eternally preexistent, the Head of the Church, the victor over death, first in all things*. On this summit we pause, looking like John, from Christ in His fullness of deity to the exhibition of that divine fullness in redemption consummated in heaven." (Vincent)

iv. The fullness is in Jesus Christ. Not in a church; not in a priesthood; not in a building; not in a sacrament; not in the saints; not in a method or a program, but *in Jesus Christ Himself*. It is in Him as a "distribution point" – so that those who wanted more of God and all that He is can find it in Jesus Christ.

l. **And by Him to reconcile all things to Himself:** Jesus' atoning work is full and broad. Yet we should not take Colossians 1:20 as an endorsement of universalism.

m. **Through the blood of the cross:** Again we notice where the peace was made. We don't make our own peace with God, but Jesus made peace for us through His work on the cross.

> i. However, we should not regard **the blood of the cross** in a superstitious manner. It is not a magical potion, nor is it the literal blood of Jesus, literally applied that saves or cleanses us. If that were so, then His Roman executioners, splattered with His blood, would have been automatically saved, and the actual number of molecules of Jesus' literal blood would limit the number of people who could be saved. The **blood of the cross** speaks to us of the real, physical death of Jesus Christ in our place, on our behalf, before God. *That literal death in our place, and the literal judgment He bore on our behalf, is what saves us.*

4. (21-23) How the greatness of Jesus' work touches the lives of the Colossians.

And you, who once were alienated and enemies in your mind by wicked works, yet now He has reconciled in the body of His flesh through death, to present you holy, and blameless, and above reproach in His sight—if indeed you continue in the faith, grounded and steadfast, and are not moved away from the hope of the gospel which you heard, which was preached to every creature under heaven, of which I, Paul, became a minister.

a. **Who once were alienated:** The ancient Greek word translated **alienated** (*apellotriomenous*) is literally "transferred to another owner." This transfer of ownership, from God to Satan and self, affected us in both *mind* and *behavior*.

> i. Belonging to the race of Adam, we are born **alienated** from God. Then as individuals, we each choose to accept and embrace that alienation with our **wicked works**.

> ii. **Once were alienated:** This means that in Jesus we are *no longer* **alienated**. The difference between a believer and a non-believer isn't merely forgiveness; there is a complete change of status.

b. **Yet now He has reconciled:** God's answer to the problem of **alienation** is *reconciliation*, initiated by His work on the cross (**reconciled in the body of His flesh through death**). In the work of reconciliation, God didn't meet us halfway. God meets us all the way and invites us to accept it.

i. One may use two different ways of understanding human need and God's salvation.

- We can see God as the judge, and we are guilty before Him. Therefore, we need forgiveness and justification.

- We can see God as our friend, and we have damaged our relationship with Him. Therefore, we need reconciliation.

ii. Both of these are true; neither one should be promoted at the expense of the other.

iii. The phrase **body of His flesh** is redundant. Paul wanted to emphasize that this happened because of something that happened to a real man on a real cross.

c. **To present you holy, and blameless, and above reproach in His sight**: This is the result of God's work of reconciliation. Taken together, these words show that in Jesus we are pure and can't even be justly accused of impurity.

i. The idea of presenting us **holy and blameless** before God may recall the terminology used when priests inspected potential sacrifices. We are presented to God as a living sacrifice.

ii. A desire to be saved means a desire to be *made* **holy, and blameless, and above reproach**; not merely a desire to escape the fires of hell on our own terms.

d. **If indeed you continue in the faith**: Those truly reconciled must truly persevere. Paul's main focus is continuing in the *truth of the gospel* (**continue in the faith... not moved away from the hope of the gospel which you heard**). It is important for Christians to continue in godly conduct, but we are not saved by our godly conduct. So it is even more important for Christians to continue in the truth of the gospel because we are saved by grace through faith.

i. "If the gospel teaches the final perseverance of the saints, it teaches at the same time that the saints are those who finally persevere - in Christ. Continuance is the test of reality." (Bruce)

C. What Paul did for the Colossians.

1. (24) Paul suffers for their sake.

I now rejoice in my sufferings for you, and fill up in my flesh what is lacking in the afflictions of Christ, for the sake of His body, which is the church,

a. **I now rejoice in my sufferings for you**: Paul wrote this from a Roman jail. He was able to see that his **sufferings** worked something good for others, so he could say that his **sufferings** were **for** the Colossians and other Christians.

b. **And fill up in my flesh what is lacking in the afflictions of Christ**: This word **afflictions** is never used for the suffering of Jesus on the cross. Most commentators see this as a reference to the affliction Jesus endured in ministry. *These* **afflictions** are not yet complete, and in this sense Jesus still "suffers" as He ministers through His people.

   i. "Paul attaches no atoning value whatever to his own sufferings for the church." (Robertson)

   ii. "The term 'afflictions of Christ' is never associated with the redemptive suffering of Jesus upon the cross. It speaks, rather, of those ministerial sufferings which Paul bears because he represents Jesus Christ." (Lane)

c. **For the sake of His body, which is the church**: Paul did not suffer for *himself* in the way that an ascetic might. Instead he suffered **for the sake of** the body of Christ.

   i. Ascetics focus on *their* holiness, on *their* spiritual growth, and on *their* perfection. Paul followed in the footsteps of Jesus and was an others-centered person. Paul found holiness, spiritual growth, and maturity when he pursued these things for others.

2. (25-26) Paul is a servant of the church, revealing the mystery of God that was once hidden.

Of which I became a minister according to the stewardship from God which was given to me for you, to fulfill the word of God, the mystery which has been hidden from ages and from generations, but now has been revealed to His saints.

   a. **Of which I became a minister**: Paul was a **minister** - that is, a *servant* of the body of Christ, the church. He did not take this position on his own initiative, but **according to the stewardship from God**. God put Paul into this position, he did not put himself.

   b. **The word of God, the mystery which has been hidden**: In the Biblical sense, a **mystery** is not a riddle. It is a truth that can only be known by revelation and not by intuition. *Now* it can be known, because it **now has been revealed to His saints**.

   i. **Hidden from ages and generations**: This reminds us that there are aspects to God's plan that *were not* clearly revealed in the Old

Testament. The specific **mystery** Paul refers to here deals with many aspects of the work of Jesus in His people, but especially the plan of the church, to make one body out of Jew and Gentile, taken from the "trunk" of Israel, yet not Israel.

ii. "The mystery is this: that God had designed to grant the Gentiles the same privileges with the Jews, and make them his people who were not his people. That this in what Paul means by the *mystery*, see Eph 3:3, etc." (Clarke)

3. (27) Part of the mystery: that Jesus would actually indwell believers.

To them God willed to make known what are the riches of the glory of this mystery among the Gentiles: which is Christ in you, the hope of glory.

a. **This mystery among the Gentiles: which is Christ in you**: The wonder and glory of the abiding, indwelling Jesus was not clearly revealed in the Old Testament, especially that He would abide in **the Gentiles**. Therefore, this aspect of the work of Jesus in His people was a **mystery** that wasn't revealed until the time of Jesus and the apostles.

i. "This is the crowning wonder to Paul that God had included the Gentiles in his redemptive grace." (Robertson)

ii. This means that God is revealed to us in Jesus. Classic theologians use the Latin term *deus absconditus* to refer to the "hidden God," the God than cannot be clearly seen or known. The Latin theological term *deus revelatus* refers to the "revealed God." In Jesus, the *deus absconditus* has become the *deus revelatus*.

b. **Christ in you, the hope of glory**: This is the Christian's **hope of glory**. It isn't our own hard work or devotion to God, or the power of our own spirituality. Instead, it is the abiding presence of Jesus: **Christ in you**.

4. (28-29) Paul's motto for apostolic ministry.

Him we preach, warning every man and teaching every man in all wisdom, that we may present every man perfect in Christ Jesus. To this *end* I also labor, striving according to His working which works in me mightily.

a. **Him we preach**: This was the focus of Paul's preaching. He didn't preach himself, or his opinions, or even lots and lots of entertaining stories. He preached *Jesus*.

b. **Warning every man and teaching every man in all wisdom**: Paul wanted the whole gospel for the whole world. He wouldn't hold back in either area – it was for **every man**, and he presented it in **all wisdom**.

i. Some translate the word **warning** as "counseling." The ancient Greek verb *nouthetountes* means, "To impart understanding," "to lay on the mind or the heart." The stress is on influencing not only the intellect, but also the will and disposition. It describes a basic means of education.

ii. The work of **warning** - or helping to impart understanding - was a passion for Paul in ministry (Acts 20:31). It is also the job of church leaders (1 Thessalonians 5:12) and of the church body in general (Colossians 3:16), providing that they are *able* to admonish others (Romans 15:14).

c. **That we may present every man perfect in Christ Jesus**: The goal of Paul's ministry was to bring people to maturity in Christ, and not to dependence upon himself.

i. "Therefore, the aim of this epistle, and, indeed, of all apostolic work is admonishing and teaching every man toward the realization of perfection in Christ, because that issues in the perfecting of the whole Church." (Morgan)

ii. This work was for **every man**. In contrast, the false teachers at Colosse "believed the way of salvation to be so involved that it could be understood only by a select few who made up sort of a spiritual aristocracy." (Vaughan)

d. **Striving according to His working which works in me mightily**: Paul's work was empowered by God's mighty strength. But God's strength in Paul's life didn't mean that he did nothing. He worked hard **according to His working**.

i. "The word 'struggling' [**striving**], whose root can mean 'to compete in the games', carries, as of then in Paul, the idea of athletic contest: Paul does not go about his work half-heartedly, hoping vaguely that grace will fill in the gaps which he is too lazy to work at himself." (Wright)

Colossians 2 - Answering the Colossian Heresy

A. Paul's conflict.

1. (1) The depth of Paul's conflict for the Colossians and others.

For I want you to know what a great conflict I have for you and those in Laodicea, and *for* as many as have not seen my face in the flesh,

> a. **What a great conflict I have for you**: This **great conflict** was *inside Paul* (**I have for you**). It wasn't that Paul fought with others about the Colossian Christians. Paul described his spiritual warfare and heartfelt care for the Colossians as a **great conflict**.

>> i. Paul used athletic imagery in Colossians 1:29 (*striving*), and he continues that sports metaphor with the words **great conflict**.

> b. **For as many as have not seen my face in the flesh**: Apparently, Paul had never visited Colosse himself. Most of the Colossian Christians had never seen his **face in the flesh**. Even as Paul's authority extended to those he had never met – to those who had never seen his face – so it also extends to us.

2. (2-3) Paul's specific concerns and goals in the spiritual conflict.

That their hearts may be encouraged, being knit together in love, and *attaining* to all riches of the full assurance of understanding, to the knowledge of the mystery of God, both of the Father and of Christ, in whom are hidden all the treasures of wisdom and knowledge.

> a. **That their hearts may be encouraged**: Paul wanted this because he was concerned about their *enthusiasm*. He knew that discouraged, downcast Christians are easy prey for the world, the flesh, and the devil.

>> i. **Encouraged**: "The word he uses is *paraklein*. Sometimes that word means to *comfort*, sometimes to *exhort*, but always at the back of it there is the idea of enabling a person to meet some difficult situation

with confidence and gallantry." (Barclay) Paul wanted these Christians to be fit for heroic action.

b. **Being knit together in love**: Paul wanted this because he was concerned about their *unity*. The unity wouldn't come from coercion, but **love**.

c. **Attaining to all riches of the full assurance of the understanding, to the knowledge of the mystery**: Paul wanted this because he was concerned about their *understanding*. He knew that their unity and steadfastness was not just a matter of **love**, but also of growing together in God's truth.

i. Paul knew that their unity came from not *only* love, but also from the truth, from both being **knit together in love** *and* growing in the **understanding** and **knowledge** of God's truth.

ii. The true wisdom Paul wanted them to know in Jesus would bring them together – indeed, **knit** them **together in love** – instead of dividing them the way that false wisdom did.

iii. For Paul, real **riches** were found in the believer's **full assurance**. Many lack **full assurance** about the character of God and are unconvinced that *He is really good and loving*. Others lack **full assurance** of their salvation and wonder if their *Christian life is for real*. Great freedom and confidence comes when we come to this **full assurance**.

d. **To the knowledge of the mystery of God**: The term **mystery of God** is used in a few different ways in the New Testament. Here, Paul uses the term regarding the character and person of God - something we could not know unless it was revealed by Him.

i. "The word 'Christ' is in the same case as 'mystery,' placing it in apposition with it. The mystery is Christ." (Wuest)

ii. "Others might lead them astray with specious talk of mysteries; but there was one mystery above all others – the mystery of God's loving purpose, disclosed in Christ alone – and Paul's concern was that they should come to know this all-surpassing mystery, and know it as an indwelling presence." (Bruce)

iii. Three mysteries are described in Colossians 1:24 through 2:3:

- The Church as the Body of Christ, for which Paul suffered and served (1:24-26).

- The Indwelling Christ, the hope of glory in each individual believer (1:27).

- The Revealed Jesus, the treasury of all wisdom and knowledge (2:2-3).

e. **Christ, in whom are hidden all the treasures of wisdom and knowledge**: This is an important idea in Paul's letter to the Colossians. With this, Paul refuted some of the bad teaching troubling the Colossian Christians. They were influenced by teachers who told them to seek the **treasures of wisdom and knowledge**, but *not* to seek them in Jesus. Paul wrote, "You will only find **all the treasures of wisdom and knowledge** in Jesus. He has them **all**." It's not wrong to seek after **wisdom and knowledge**; but we must seek it all in Jesus.

> i. When Paul said this wisdom is **hidden** in Christ, he used the ancient Greek word *apokruphos*. "His very use of that word is a blow aimed at the Gnostics.... Gnostics believed that a great mass of elaborate knowledge was necessary for salvation. That knowledge they set down in their books which they called *apokruphos* because they were barred to the ordinary man." (Barclay) Paul wanted all to know that real **wisdom** was not hidden in secret books, but deposited in Jesus Christ so that all can access it.

> ii. "'Hidden' does not, however, mean that they are concealed but rather that they are laid up or stored away as a treasure." (Vaughn)

> iii. "Everything we might want to ask about God and his purposes can and must now be answered – this is the force of the verse – with reference to the crucified and risen Jesus, the Messiah." (Wright)

> iv. "He is indeed the Mystery of God, profound in the wonder of His being, and yet so real that the tiniest child talks of Him with sweet familiarity." (Morgan)

> v. When Paul describes the truth of God with words like **riches** and **treasures**, he reminds us that God's truth is precious and worthy of sacrificial seeking.

3. (4) Paul's earnest warning.

Now this I say lest anyone should deceive you with persuasive words.

a. **Lest anyone should deceive you with persuasive words**: Those who told the Colossians to find wisdom and knowledge apart from the simplicity of Jesus were very **persuasive**. The lure of "hidden" and "deep" wisdom and knowledge can be both strong and deceptive.

b. **Lest anyone should deceive you**: Paul did not say that they had *already* been deceived, but he clearly saw the danger and warned them about it.

> i. It might sound simple, but deceivers are deceivers. They won't announce their false doctrine as false doctrine, and it will often be similar enough to the truth to be dangerous.

4. (5-7) Paul's confidence in their present standing.

For though I am absent in the flesh, yet I am with you in spirit, rejoicing to see your *good* order and the steadfastness of your faith in Christ. As you have therefore received Christ Jesus the Lord, so walk in Him, rooted and built up in Him and established in the faith, as you have been taught, abounding in it with thanksgiving.

a. **I am absent in the flesh, yet I am with you in spirit**: Through prayer – the core of his *conflict* mentioned in Colossians 2:1 – Paul genuinely felt he was among the Colossian Christians **in spirit**, even though he was **absent in the flesh**.

i. "Paul's sense of being spiritually present with his absent friends could be extraordinarily strong and vivid. Perhaps the most remarkable example is found in 1 Corinthians 5:3-5, where he speaks of himself as present in spirit at a church meeting in Corinth (at a time when he was resident in Ephesus)." (Bruce)

b. **Rejoicing to see your good order**: Continuing with the thought from the previous verse, Paul did not see a Colossian church that was given over to heresy. They were under serious danger, but they were still in **good order** and displayed the **steadfastness of** their **faith**.

i. According to Vaughn, the words **order** and **steadfastness** are both military words. "He sees the situation of the Colossians as being like that of an army under attack and affirms that their lines were unbroken, their discipline intact, and their 'faith in Christ' unshaken."

c. **As you have therefore received Christ Jesus the Lord, so walk in Him**: This is a wonderful rule for Christian living. We cannot perfect in the flesh what was begun in the Spirit; therefore just as you **received** Jesus, **walk in Him** in the same way. The simple things of the Christian life provide continual and reliable spiritual fuel for growth. We always have to be reminded of the **things we have been taught**.

i. "When he says that they have 'received' Christ Jesus as their Lord, he uses the verb which was specifically employed to denote the receiving of something which was delivered by tradition. In other words, the Colossians have received Christ himself as their 'tradition,' and this should prove a sufficient safeguard against following the 'tradition of men' (Colossians 2:8)." (Bruce)

ii. "That is, Paul is speaking of the doctrines regarding the Person and Work of the Lord Jesus, rather than of Him personally, for the former were involved in the Colossian heresy." (Wuest)

iii. "He does not receive his qualities and attributes [of holiness] as things apart from the Lord Jesus; but receiving Him, he obtains them. The holy man is he who has learned the art of receiving Jesus." (Meyer)

d. **So walk in Him, rooted and built up**: Paul used a curious combination of metaphors. As Christians, we **walk**, but we are also **rooted**, and we are also **built up**. The metaphors are somewhat mixed, but the message is clear: be established and keep growing.

i. "It is not usual with the apostle to employ this double metaphor, taken partly from the *growth of a tree* and the *increase of a building*. They are to be *rooted*; as the good *seed* had been already *sown*, it is to take root, and the roots are to spread far, wide, and deep. They are to be *grounded*; as the *foundation* has already been *laid*, they are to *build* thereon. In the one case, they are to bear much fruit; in the other, they are to grow up to be a habitation of God through the Spirit." (Clarke)

B. Paul warns against and exposes the Colossian heresy.

1. (8) A warning: Don't be cheated by philosophies and traditions.

Beware lest anyone cheat you through philosophy and empty deceit, according to the tradition of men, according to the basic principles of the world, and not according to Christ.

a. **Beware lest anyone cheat you through philosophy**: The false teaching among the Colossians was marked by an emphasis on **philosophy and empty deceit**. Most of all, it was **according to the tradition of men**. It had the stamp of *man* on it, not *God*.

i. Peake says the best sense of the phrase **cheat you** is actually, "lead you away as prey." It also had the ideas of robbing and plundering. "Their goods were the salvation they had received from Christ; and both the Gentile and Jewish teachers endeavoured to deprive them of these, by perverting their minds, and leading them off from the truths of Christianity." (Clarke)

ii. This **philosophy** that threatened the Colossian Christians was a strange ecclectic mix of early Gnosticism, Greek philosophy, local mystery religions, and Jewish mysticism. The philosophy threatening the Colossian Christians was so dangerous because it was not obviously sinful and licentious. It was high-sounding and seemed highly intelligent.

iii. Vincent on the word **philosophy**: "It had originally a good meaning, *the love of wisdom*, but is used by Paul in the sense of *vain speculation*, and with special reference to its being the name by which the false teachers at Colossae designated not only their speculative system, but also their practical system, so that it covered their ascetic practices no less than mysticism."

iv. There is significant debate among commentators as to the exact nature of the Colossian heresy. Some see it as predominately an expression of early Gnosticism with some Jewish mystical elements added; others see it as primarily Jewish mysticism with a few aspects of early Gnosticism. Whatever the exact origin or composition of this heresy, it seems clear that it had both elements.

v. The connection to early Gnosticism is clear from the way Paul brings forth his points.

- Gnosticism taught that God (as a Perfect Spirit) could not come into direct contact with the material world. Paul took care to point out that Jesus is God, and He came *in the body of His flesh* (Colossians 1:19-22).

- Gnosticism taught that since God could not have direct contact with the material world, that God Himself did not create the world, but He worked through lesser spirits or angels. Paul took care to show that Jesus was the creator of the world (Colossians 1:15-16).

- Gnosticism (and some forms of Jewish mysticism) taught that God did not deal directly with man and the material world, but that He dealt with the world through a series of mediators. Paul took care to show that Jesus did the work of reconciliation Himself (Colossians 1:19-20).

- Gnosticism (and some forms of Jewish mysticism) greatly esteemed these supposed mediators, and considered them angelic beings of a sort. Paul was careful to warn the Colossians that angels should not be worshipped (Colossians 2:18).

vi. The connection to Jewish mysticism is clear from the way Paul brings forth a few more points.

- Jewish influence on Christianity emphasized dietary laws. Paul took care to say that Christians were not under Jewish dietary laws (Colossians 2:16).

- Jewish influence on Christianity emphasized the observance of particular days as an obligation. Paul took care to say that Christians were not under these obligations (Colossians 2:16).

b. **According to the tradition of men**: The Colossian heresy promoted itself as *traditional*. It could trace some or many of its ideas back to traditions among the Jews or the Greek philosophers or both. Paul here warned that **the tradition of men** has no equal authority to the word of God.

c. **According to the basic principles of the world**: The ancient Greek word translated **basic principles** is *stoicheia*. It is a word that can mean several different things based on their context, and Paul may have used such a broad word to cover a variety of meanings.

> i. "The noun *stoicheia* means primarily things placed side by side in a row; it is used of the letters of the alphabet, the ABCs, and then, since learning one's ABCs is the first lesson in a literary education, it comes to mean 'rudiments,' 'first principles' (cf. Hebrews 5:12, as the 'rudiments' of the gospel)." (Bruce) Because of this association with fundamental elements, the word came to also refer to basic elements such as earth, water, air, and fire.

> ii. Many ancient mystery religions thought of the world as a dangerous place, threatened by spirits or spiritual forces they called *elements* or *elemental forces* (such as Paul uses the word in Colossians 2:8 and 2:20). They thought one was protected from these dangerous spiritual forces by either worshipping them or by finding protection under a greater deity or spiritual power that was superior to these *elements*.

> iii. Yet, one might say that Paul's meaning here certainly *includes* an answer to early Gnostic ideas, but the meaning also goes beyond those specific ideas. "It has been frequently taken in this sense as the ABC of religious knowledge... the expression must apply to something both [Jews and pagans] had in common." (Peake)

> iv. Common to both Jews and pagans was the basic idea of *cause and effect* and in a sense it rules nature and the minds of men. We live under the idea that we get what we deserve; when we are good, we deserve to receive good; when we are bad, we deserve to receive bad. Paul warned the Colossians to not subject themselves to this grace-eliminating kind of thinking, and to consider themselves dead to it.

2. (9-10) The completeness of Jesus and our connection with Him shows other philosophies and traditions are unnecessary.

For in Him dwells all the fullness of the Godhead bodily; and you are complete in Him, who is the head of all principality and power.

a. **In Him dwells all the fullness of the Godhead**: This is a dramatic, airtight declaration of the full Deity of Jesus. Since **all the fullness of the Godhead** dwells in Jesus, He cannot be a halfway God or a junior god.

> i. **Godhead**: "Paul is declaring that in the Son there dwells all the fullness of absolute Godhead; they were no mere rays of divine glory

which gilded Him, lighting up His Person for a season and with splendor not His own; but He was, and is, absolute and perfect God; and the apostle uses *theotes* to express this essential and personal Godhead of the Son." (Trench, cited in Wuest)

b. **All the fullness of the Godhead bodily**: The false teaching among the Colossian Christians was something like an early form of the Gnostic heresies that would come later. These Gnostic heresies made a radical separation between the *spiritual* and the *material*. That is why Paul needed to make it clear that **all the fullness of the Godhead** was in Jesus **bodily**, not in some strange, mystical sense. John also dealt with this false teaching in 1 John 4:2-3 and other passages.

i. A false teaching related to this in the early church was called *Docetism*, which claimed that Jesus had no actual human body; He only *seemed* to have one. Another false teaching was called *Cerinthianism*, and it said that "Jesus the man" was separate and distinct from "the Spirit of Christ."

c. **And you are complete in Him**: This can only be true because Jesus is truly God. If He were not God, we couldn't be **complete** in Him. Anything that says we are *not* **complete in Him** also takes away from the deity of Jesus.

i. If all the fullness of God dwells in Jesus, and as believers we are united to Him in a faith-relationship, then *we* are also **complete in Him**. Therefore there was no need to go to the false promises and attractions presented by the false teachers among the Colossians.

ii. **You *are* complete in Him**: Paul says that this is a fact to be enjoyed, not a status to be achieved.

d. **Head of all principality and power**: In many New Testament passages, **principality and power** describes ranks of angelic beings, either faithful or fallen angelic beings (Romans 8:38, Ephesians 1:21, Ephesians 3:10, Ephesians 6:12). Therefore, Paul here declares Jesus' authority over all spirit beings. The false teaching among the Colossian Christians emphasized these lesser spirit beings, but Paul makes it clear that Jesus is far above them.

3. (11-12) The work of Jesus in His people through spiritual circumcision and illustrated by baptism.

In Him you were also circumcised with the circumcision made without hands, by putting off the body of the sins of the flesh, by the circumcision of Christ, buried with Him in baptism, in which you also were raised

with *Him* through faith in the working of God, who raised Him from the dead.

a. **In Him you were also circumcised**: Most of the Colossian Christians were Gentiles who had never been physically circumcised. Paul assures them that they **were** indeed circumcised in a spiritual sense, which is even more important than physical circumcision.

i. The Colossian Christians had to deal with a whole variety of false teaching. Not only did they have wrong ideas about Jesus, but they also had wrong ideas about things like circumcision. Apparently, they were being taught that they had to be circumcised to be right with God. Paul makes it clear that they *were* circumcised, **by putting off the sins of the flesh**.

ii. "It seems probable that the false teachers set a high value on circumcision, and urged it on the Colossians, not as indispensable to salvation, in which case Paul would have definitely attacked them on this point, but as conferring higher sanctity." (Peake)

iii. Our spiritual circumcision meant the **putting off** of the old man. "The Greek word for 'putting off', a double compound, denotes both stripping off and casting away. The imagery is that of discarding – or being divested of – a piece of filthy clothing." (Vaughn)

iv. **You were also circumcised**: "A definite historical fact is referred to, as is shown by the aorist [verb tense]. This was their conversion, the inward circumcision of the heart, by which they entered on the blessings of the New Covenant." (Peake)

b. **By the circumcision of Christ, buried with Him in baptism**: Paul says these Gentile Christians find their true **circumcision** in their **baptism**. Christians don't need to be circumcised, they need to be baptized.

i. Even the Old Testament acknowledges that there are two types of circumcision: one of the body and one of the heart (Deuteronomy 10:16 and 30:6; Jeremiah 4:4 and 9:25; Ezekiel 44:7 and 44:9). Sincere baptism shows that the real "circumcision of the heart" has taken place.

c. **Buried with Him in baptism, in which you also were raised with Him through faith in the working of God**: Baptism *answers* circumcision, but it doesn't *illustrate* it. Yet baptism does illustrate our identification with the death and resurrection life of Jesus. We were **buried** with Jesus, and **buried** under the water. We are also **raised with Him**, and raised up out of the water.

i. It is as if Paul wrote: "Circumcision is not important; what is important is the spiritual cutting away of the flesh that Jesus performs in the life of every believer. If you want a ceremony to mark this spiritual transformation in your life, look to your baptism and not to circumcision."

ii. Because Paul made a connection here between circumcision and baptism, some - especially Reformed theologians - say that just as babies were circumcised, so babies should be baptized. But this presses Paul's analogy between circumcision and baptism too far and neglects examples of baptism in the Book of Acts. Paul doesn't say that circumcision and baptism are the same thing, but that circumcision is unnecessary for salvation because we are identified in Jesus and we are baptized to show that.

iii. "The emphasis of the verse, however, is not on the analogy between circumcision and baptism; that concept, though implied, is soon dismissed, and the thought shifts to that of baptism as symbolizing the believer's participation in the burial and resurrection of Christ." (Vaughn)

iv. **Through faith in the working of God**: This demonstrates that Paul understood that the power of regeneration was not in baptism or received by the act of baptism, but received **through faith in the working of God**.

4. (13-15) The work of Jesus in His people through His work on the cross.

And you, being dead in your trespasses and the uncircumcision of your flesh, He has made alive together with Him, having forgiven you all trespasses, having wiped out the handwriting of requirements that was against us, which was contrary to us. And He has taken it out of the way, having nailed it to the cross. Having disarmed principalities and powers, He made a public spectacle of them, triumphing over them in it.

a. **And you, being dead**: This is the place of every person before they *are raised with Him through faith in the working of God* as Paul described in Colossians 2:12. Before we have new life, we are **dead**. The Bible has many descriptions of men and women apart from Jesus Christ, and this is one of the strongest. A sick person may need a doctor, but a **dead** person needs a Savior.

i. We are not only **made alive**, but **made alive together with Him**. "It is true that He gave us life from the dead? He gave us pardon of sin; He gave us imputed righteousness. These are all precious things, but you see we are not content with them; we have received *Christ himself.* The Son of God has been poured out into us, and we have received him, and appropriated him." (Spurgeon)

b. **Being dead in your trespasses and the uncircumcision of your flesh**: Before we have new life in Jesus, we are dead **in** our **trespasses**. A trespass is a specific kind of sin: overstepping a boundary. We are dead because we overstep God's boundaries in our sin and rebellion.

c. **He has made alive together with Him**: We can't make ourselves alive, but God can make us **alive together with** Jesus. We can never be **made alive** apart from Jesus.

   i. The new birth (**made alive**) and cleansing (**forgiven you all**) go together as features of the New Covenant, as prophesied by the Old Testament (Ezekiel 36:25-27) and the New Testament (John 3:5).

   ii. **Having forgiven us** is the ancient Greek word *charizomai* - a verb form of the ancient Greek word *charis* (grace). We are forgiven by grace.

d. **Having wiped out the handwriting of requirements that was against us**: The **handwriting of requirements** has in mind a list of our crimes or moral debt before God, a debt that no imperfect person can completely pay. But it can be **taken out of the way**, by payment from a perfect man, Jesus Christ.

   i. The term **handwriting** is a general word for a handwritten document and has been understood in various ways. Some take it in a *legal* sense and say it represents the charges against a prisoner, or a confession of wrong made by a prisoner. Others take it in a *financial* sense and see it as a debit or ledger sheet that shows we are bankrupt before God. Either way, it means that the document that once condemned us is now taken out of the way, having been nailed to the cross.

   ii. "Each of the ten commandments has, as it were, united with the rest to draw up an indictment against us. The first commandment says, 'He has broken me.' The second cries, 'He has broken me,' — the third, 'He has broken me;' and the whole ten together have laid the same charge against each one of us; that is the handwriting of the law condemning every man of woman born while he remains in a state of nature." (Spurgeon)

   iii. "It might even be said that he took the document, ordinances and all, and nailed it to his cross as an act of triumphant defiance in the face of those blackmailing powers that were holding it over men and women in order to command their allegiance." (Bruce)

iv. According to Vincent, the ancient Greek word translated **wiped out** is a compound of the word *to anoint* and the prefix that means *completely*. The idea is that something was *completely wiped over*, and in the ancient world the term was used of whitewashing a wall, or overlaying a wall with gold. It means that the accusations against us were completely wiped away and covered over.

e. **Having nailed it to the cross**: Jesus not only *paid* for the writing that was against us; He also took **it out of the way**, and then **nailed it to the cross**. He did everything possible to make certain that the **handwriting of requirements that was against us** could no longer accuse us.

i. "Paul, looking at the cross, saw there instead the *titulus* that expressed the charge against all Jesus' people, the written code that stood over against them, disqualifying them from the life of the new age. And it was God, not Pilate, that put it there." (Wright)

ii. We remember that the accusations of Jesus' crime were nailed to the cross and hung above His head (Matthew 27:37). Since we are identified with Jesus in His death on the cross (Romans 6:3-8), it is as if the **handwriting of requirements that was against us** was also nailed to the cross, just like the accusation against Jesus.

f. **Having disarmed principalities and powers**: Another aspect of Jesus' work on the cross is that He **disarmed principalities and powers**. These ranks of hostile angelic beings (Romans 8:38, Ephesians 1:21, Ephesians 3:10, Ephesians 6:12) don't have the same weapons to use against Christians that they have against those who are not in Jesus.

i. The greatest powers of the earth at that time – Rome, the greatest governmental power and Judaism, the greatest religious power – conspired together to put the Son of God on the cross. "These powers, angry at his challenge to their sovereignty, stripped *him* naked, held *him* up to public contempt, and celebrated a triumph over *him*." (Wright) Here Paul shows us again the paradox of the cross; that the victorious Jesus took the spiritual powers animating these earthly powers and stripped *them*, held *them* up to contempt, and publicly triumphed over *them*.

ii. We can only imagine how Satan and every dark gleeful demon attacked Jesus as He hung on the cross on our behalf, as if He were a guilty sinner. "As he was suspended there, bound hand and foot to the wood in apparent weakness, they imagined they had him at their mercy, and flung themselves on him with hostile intent. But, far from suffering their attack without resistance, he grappled with them and mastered them, stripping them of the armor in which they trusted, and held them aloft in his outstretched hands, displaying to the universe their helplessness and his own unvanquished strength." (Bruce)

iii. Paul wrote in another place that if the rulers of this age – by which he meant both the spiritual powers of darkness and their earthly representatives – had known what would happen on the cross, they would have never crucified Jesus (1 Corinthians 2:8). They were defeating themselves and they didn't even know it.

iv. Against the believer, what weapons do demonic spirits therefore now have? They are **disarmed**, except for their ability to *deceive* and to create *fear*. These are effective "weapons" that are not tangible weapons at all. Demonic spirits only have power towards us that we grant them by believing their lies. The weapons are in *our* hands, not *theirs*. We will one-day see how afraid they were of *us*.

g. **Triumphing over them**: Paul used similar phrasing in 2 Corinthians 2:14, where he had in mind the Roman victory parade where a conquering general led his defeated captives through the streets in triumph.

i. Perhaps Satan, for a moment, thought that he had won at the cross. But Hell's imagined victory was turned into a defeat that **disarmed** every spiritual enemy who fights against those living under the light and power of the cross. The **public spectacle of** defeated demonic spirits makes their defeat all the more humiliating.

ii. "Christ, in this picture, is the conquering general; the powers and authorities are the vanquished enemy displayed as the spoils of battle before the entire universe." (Vaughn)

iii. "The death of Christ was not only a pardon; it also manifested might. It not only canceled a debt; it was a glorious triumph." (Erdman)

5. (16-17) Applying the truth of Jesus' victory in light of the Colossian heresy.

So let no one judge you in food or in drink, or regarding a festival or a new moon or sabbaths, which are a shadow of things to come, but the substance is of Christ.

a. **So let no one judge you**: The opening "**so**" is important. It connects this thought with the previous thought. *Because* Jesus won such a glorious victory on the cross, we are to **let no one judge you in food or in drink** or in other matters related to legalism. A life that is centered on Jesus and what He did on the cross has no place for legalism.

i. "It would be preposterous indeed for those who had reaped the benefit of Christ's victory to put themselves voluntarily under the control of the powers which he had conquered." (Bruce)

b. **Food or in drink, or regarding a festival or a new moon or sabbaths, which are a shadow of things to come**: The Old Testament law had certain provisions that are done away with in Jesus, regarding such things as **food** and **sabbaths**. It isn't that those laws were *bad*, simply that they were **a shadow of things to come**. Once the **substance** - Jesus Christ - has come, we don't need to **shadow** any more.

i. The point is clear: days and foods, as observed under the Mosaic Law, are not binding upon New Covenant people. The shadow has passed, the reality has come. So for the Christian, *all* foods are pure (1 Timothy 4:4-5) and *all* days belong to God.

ii. Christians are therefore free to keep a kosher diet or to observe the sabbath if they please. There is nothing wrong with those things. However, they cannot think that eating kosher or sabbath observance makes them any closer to God, and they cannot **judge** another brother or sister who does not observe such laws.

iii. "The regulations of Judaism were designed for the period when the people of God consisted of one racial, cultural, and geographical unit, and are simply put out of date now that this people is becoming a world-wide family. They were the 'shadows' that the approaching new age casts before it." (Wright)

6. (18-19) Paul rebukes the strange mysticism of the Colossian heresy.

Let no one cheat you of your reward, taking delight in *false* humility and worship of angels, intruding into those things which he has not seen, vainly puffed up by his fleshly mind, and not holding fast to the Head, from whom all the body, nourished and knit together by joints and ligaments, grows with the increase *that is* from God.

a. **Taking delight in false humility and worship of angels**: These aspects of **false humility** and the **worship of angels** were parts of the false teaching troubling the Colossian Christians. That is why Paul touches back on these themes throughout the letter of Colossians. The antidote for both of these false teachings is simply more of Jesus, exalting Him above **angels**, and realizing that because of His finished work there is nothing to take pride in.

i. "That is to say, the heretics probably insisted that their worship of angels rather than the supreme God was an expression of humility on their part." (Vaughn)

ii. "Their humility found an expression in angel worship. It is therefore that lowliness which causes a man to think himself unworthy to come into fellowship with God, and therefore prompts to worship of the angels." (Peake)

b. **False humility** and the **worship of angels** do not make anyone more spiritual. Instead, **holding fast to the Head** (Jesus) makes us truly spiritual.

c. **Intruding into those things which he has not seen, vainly puffed up by his fleshly mind, and not holding fast to the Head**: This describes the spiritual arrogance of these false teachers and those who believed what they taught. There are few things more dangerous among Christians than spiritual pride and arrogance.

> i. **Intruding into those things which he has not seen**: "That is a mistranslation. The correct translation should be 'making a parade of things which he has seen.' The Gnostic prided himself upon the special visions of secret things which were not open to the eyes of ordinary men and women." (Barclay)

> ii. **Vainly puffed up**: "*Vainly* characterizes the emptiness of such pretension; *puffed up*, the swelling intellectual pride of those who make it. The humility is thus characterized as affected, and the teachers as charlatans." (Vincent)

d. **From whom all the body**: When these strange, mystical movements arise in the church, they don't appeal to the *whole body*, but only to a few "elite" Christians. This is not the cause under **the Head**, Jesus - He wants **all the body** to grow together.

e. **Grows with the increase which is from God**: This is God's plan for church growth. We remain faithful and connected to Jesus (our **Head**), and God gives the increase.

7. (20-23) Paul rebukes the essence of legalism.

Therefore, if you died with Christ from the basic principles of the world, why, as *though* living in the world, do you subject yourselves to regulations—"Do not touch, do not taste, do not handle," which all concern things which perish with the using—according to the commandments and doctrines of men? These things indeed have an appearance of wisdom in self-imposed religion, *false* humility, and neglect of the body, *but are* of no value against the indulgence of the flesh.

a. **Do not... do not... do not**: This is a perfect description of legalistic religion, defined more by what we *don't do* than by what we *do*. Christianity is a moral religion; it does have clear moral boundaries. But at its foundation, Christianity is a religion of *positive action*.

b. **You died with Christ from the basic principles of the world**: Remembering this is the key to living above legalism. Our identification with Jesus in both His death and resurrection (as mentioned before in

Colossians 2:12) becomes the foundation for our Christian life, instead of our law-keeping.

i. **Which perish with the using**: "They are things which come to an end in the very act of being used. Handling them, eating them, or the like involves their destruction. Food, once eaten, ceases to be food. These are not the things that matter most; these are not the ultimate realities." (Bruce)

c. **According to the commandments and doctrines of men**: One aspect of legalism is that the **doctrines of men** are promoted as the laws of God.

d. **These things indeed have an appearance of wisdom... but are of no value against the indulgence of the flesh**: We might regard this as the greatest indictment against legalism in the Bible. At the bottom line, legalism's rules have no value in restraining the **indulgence of the flesh**.

i. All such legalistic rules may have an **appearance** of wisdom, but they have no real value. Legalism doesn't restrain the flesh; it *feeds* the flesh in a subtle, powerful way. "In fact, the most rigorous asceticism can coexist with insufferable spiritual pride, one of the subtlest and most intractable of the 'works of the flesh.'" (Bruce)

ii. **Self-imposed religion** is man reaching to God, trying to justify himself by keeping a list of rules. Christianity is God reaching down to man in love through Christ.

Colossians 3 - Put Off, Put On

A. Put off the old man.

1. (1-4) The basis for Paul's practical instruction.

If then you were raised with Christ, seek those things which are above, where Christ is, sitting at the right hand of God. Set your mind on things above, not on things on the earth. For you died, and your life is hidden with Christ in God. When Christ *who is* our life appears, then you also will appear with Him in glory.

> a. **If then you were raised with Christ**: Paul here begins a section where he focuses on practical Christian living, with the clear understanding that practical Christian living is built on the foundation of theological truth. Because we know that Jesus is really raised from the dead, then our identification with Him becomes real. It is only because we **were raised with Christ** that we can **seek those things which are above**.

> > i. The idea of being **raised with Christ** was introduced back in Colossians 2:12, where Paul used baptism to illustrate this spiritual reality. Now, seeing that we are **raised with Christ**, certain behavior is appropriate to us.

> > ii. "The opening verses of chapter 3 sustain the closest connection with the closing verses of chapter 2. There the apostle reminds the Colossians that ascetic regulations are of no real value in restraining indulgence of the flesh. The only remedy for sinful passions is found in the believers' experience of union with Christ." (Vaughan)

> > iii. Because we **were raised with Christ**, we should act just as Jesus did when He was resurrected.

> > > • After His resurrection, Jesus left the tomb. So should we – we don't live there any more.

- After His resurrection, Jesus spent His remaining time being with and ministering to His disciples. So should we – live our lives to be with and to serve one another.

- After His resurrection, Jesus lived in supernatural power with the ability to do impossible things. So should we – with the power and the enabling of the Holy Spirit.

- After His resurrection, Jesus looked forward to heaven, knowing He would soon enough ascend there. So should we – recognizing that our citizenship is in heaven.

iv. To emphasize it even more, Paul added the phrase, **sitting at the right hand of God**: "This phrase, particularly in its allusion to Psalm 110, focuses attention on the sovereign rule which Christ now exercises. The command to aspire to the things of heaven is a command to meditate and dwell upon Christ's sort of life, and on the fact that he is now enthroned as the Lord of the world." (Wright)

b. **Set your mind on things above**: The best Christian living comes from minds that are fixed on *heaven*. They realize that their lives are now **hidden with Christ in God**, and since Jesus is enthroned in heaven, their thoughts and hearts are connected to heaven also.

i. "The believer is to 'seek the things... above.' The word 'seek' marks aspiration, desire, and passion... In order to seek these things the mind must be set on them." (Morgan)

ii. "Love *heavenly things*; *study* them; let your hearts be entirely *engrossed* by them. Now, that you are converted to God, act in reference to heavenly things as ye did formerly in reference to those of earth." (Clarke)

iii. "'Earthly things' are not all evil, but some of them are. Even things harmless in themselves become harmful if permitted to take the place that should be reserved for the things above." (Vaughan)

c. **When Christ who is our life appears, then you also will appear with Him in glory**: The promise of the return of Jesus is not only that we will see *His* glory, but so that we also **will appear with Him in glory**. This is the *revealing of the sons of God* mentioned in Romans 8:19

i. **Christ who is our life**: In another place, Paul wrote *For me to live is Christ* (Philippians 1:21). Here he shows that this idea was not just for special apostles, but for all believers – **Christ who is our life**. Sometimes we say, "Music is his life" or "Sports is his life" or "He lives for his work." Of the Christian it should be said, "Jesus Christ is his life."

ii. On that day, all will see the saints of God for what they *really are*, not as they merely appear to this world. "Paul, the prisoner, an eccentric Jew to the Romans and a worse-than-Gentile traitor to the Jews, will be seen as Paul the apostle, the servant of the King. The Colossians, insignificant ex-pagans from a third-rate country town, will be seen in a glory which, if it were now to appear, one might be tempted to worship." (Wright)

2. (5-7) Put to death the things that are against God and part of this world.

Therefore put to death your members which are on the earth: fornication, uncleanness, passion, evil desire, and covetousness, which is idolatry. Because of these things the wrath of God is coming upon the sons of disobedience, in which you yourselves once walked when you lived in them.

a. **Therefore put to death your members: Therefore** points back to our identification with the risen and enthroned Lord Jesus mentioned in Colossians 3:1-4. It is because we understand this fact that we can **put to death** the things in our life that are contrary to our identity with Jesus.

i. "The verb *nekrosate*, meaning literally 'to make dead,' is very strong. It suggests that we are not simply to suppress or control evil acts and attitudes. We are to wipe them out, completely exterminate the old way of life." (Vaughan)

ii. We **put to death** in the sense of denying these things and considering them dead to us and us dead to them. "To *gratify* any sensual appetite is to give it the very food and nourishment by which it lives, thrives, and is active." (Clarke)

iii. There is importance in *listing* and *naming* these sins as Paul does in this section. "It is far easier to drift into a sin which one does not know by name than consciously to choose one whose very title should be repugnant to a Christian." (Wright)

b. **Fornication, uncleanness, passion** and **evil desire**: Each of these terms refers to sexual sins. **Covetousness** is simple, but insidious greed, and nothing less than **idolatry**. There is no way that Jesus would walk in any of these sins, so if we identify with Him, we won't walk in them either.

i. **Fornication**: "The word here translated *sexual immorality* refers to any intercourse outside marriage; in the ancient world, as in the modern, intercourse with a prostitute would be a specific, and in a pagan culture a frequent, instance of this." (Wright)

ii. **Uncleanness**: "A wider range of meaning than fornication. It includes the misuse of sex, but is applicable to various forms of moral evil." (Bruce)

iii. Morgan lists three ways that covetousness is terribly destructive:

- "First, it is idolatry, in that it only obtains when man thinks of life consisting in things possessed, rather than in righteous relationship to God."

- "It is also a sin against others, for to satisfy the desire, others are wronged."

- "Finally, it is self-destructive, for these wrong conceptions and activities always react upon the soul to its own undoing."

- Morgan added: "And yet, what ecclesiastical court ever yet arraigned a church-member for covetousness?"

iv. "Every godly man seeks his happiness in God; the covetous man seeks that in his money which God alone can give; therefore his covetousness is properly *idolatry*." (Clarke)

c. **Because of these things**: The sins mentioned previously are part of the way the world lives and not the way Jesus lives. Every Christian is faced with a question: "Who will I identify with, the world or with Jesus?"

d. **The wrath of God is coming upon the sons of disobedience**: These sins invite **the wrath of God**. Because the world loves this kind of sinful lifestyle, they don't come in humility to Jesus. As they continue in these sins, it adds to their condemnation. One sin is enough to send anyone to hell (James 2:10), but there are greater levels of condemnation (Matthew 23:14).

i. In part, **the wrath of God** comes as God allows men to continue in sinful - and therefore self-destructive - behavior (as in Romans 1:24-32).

e. **In which you yourselves once walked when you lived in them**: These sins may mark a world in rebellion against God, but they are in the *past tense* for the Christian.

i. Simply put, the Christian should not live like the **sons of disobedience**. A true Christian can not be comfortable in habitual sin.

ii. Paul says that Christians **once walked** in these sins. It is possible - though tragic - that these sins should *occasionally* mark a Christian's life, but they must not be a Christian's **walk**, their manner of living.

3. (8-9) Removing other traces of worldliness.

But now you yourselves are to put off all these: anger, wrath, malice, blasphemy, filthy language out of your mouth. Do not lie to one another, since you have put off the old man with his deeds,

a. **But now you yourselves are to put off all these**: The sins Paul next lists (**anger, wrath**, and so forth) are regarded by many as "little" sins that Christians may overlook with little danger. Paul challenges us to **put off** the old man in *every* area of our lives.

i. "Put off all those old habits, just as you would discard an outworn suit of clothes which no longer fitted you." (Bruce)

b. **Anger, wrath, malice, blasphemy, filthy language out of your mouth. Do not lie**: Each of these sins are primarily committed by what we *say*. When Paul calls the believer to a deeper obedience, he tells us to *bridle* our *tongue* (as did James in James 1:26 and 3:1-9).

i. Nevertheless, it is also possible to **lie to one another** without words. "It is easy to distort the truth; an alteration in the tone of voice or an eloquent look will do it; and there are silences which can be as false and misleading as any words." (Barclay)

c. **Since you have put off the old man with his deeds**: The more notorious sins of Colossians 3:5 are easily seen as incompatible with the nature of Jesus. But these "lesser" sins are also incompatible, so **put off** these sins also.

i. In this section (Colossians 3:5-9) Paul showed two high priorities in Christian living: sexual morality connected with a right attitude towards material things, *and* simple getting along in love with one another. It is easy for a Christian community to compromise one for the other, but Paul (by inspiration of the Holy Spirit) insisted that they *both* have a high place in Christian practice.

ii. **You have put off the old man with his deeds** means that in Jesus Christ, the saints of God are *different people*. Therefore, "When a tide of passion or a surge of anger is felt, it must be dealt with as the alien intruder it really is, and turned out of the house as having no right to be there at all, let alone to be giving orders." (Wright)

B. Put on the new man.

1. (10-11) As we put off the old man, we must put on the new man.

And have put on the new *man* who is renewed in knowledge according to the image of Him who created him, where there is neither Greek

nor Jew, circumcised nor uncircumcised, barbarian, Scythian, slave *nor* free, but Christ *is* all and in all.

a. **Put on the new man**: The phrase Paul used was commonly used for changing a set of clothes. We can almost picture a person taking off the old and putting on the **new man** in Jesus.

b. **Who is renewed in knowledge**: Because the new man is **renewed in knowledge**, he is hungry to know what *God says* in His Word.

c. **According to the image of Him who created him**: Paul is clearly alluding to Genesis 1:27, where it is said that God created Adam in His own image. Nevertheless, now that the first Adam is regarded as the **old man** who should be put off and discarded, because now we are created after the **image** of the *second* Adam, Jesus Christ.

d. **Where there is neither Greek nor Jew, circumcised nor uncircumcised, barbarian, Scythian, slave nor free**: The new man is part of a family, which favors no race, nationality, class, culture or ethnicity. It only favors Jesus, because in this new family, **Christ is all and in all**.

i. This work of the new creation not only deals with the old man and gives us the new man patterned after Jesus Christ; it also breaks down the barriers that separate people in society. Among new creation people it doesn't matter if one is **Greek** or **Jew** or **circumcised** or **uncircumcised** or a **Scythian** or a **slave** or a **free** man. All those barriers are broken down.

ii. "He therefore adds to barbarian the Scythian as the extreme example." (Peake)

iii. All of these barriers existed in the ancient Roman world; and the power of God through the Gospel of Jesus Christ broke them all down. Especially powerful was the barrier between **slave** and **free**, but Christianity changed that.

iv. "In times of persecution slaves showed that they could face the trial and suffer for their faith as courageously as freeborn Romans. The slave-girl Blandina and her mistress both suffered in the persecution which broke out against the churches of the Rhone valley in A.D. 177, but it was the slave-girl who was the hero of the persecution, impressing friend and foe alike as a 'noble athlete' in the contest of martyrdom." (Bruce)

v. "In the arena of Carthage in A.D. 202 a profound impression was made on the spectators when the Roman matron Perpetua stood hand-in-hand with her slave Felicitas, as both women faced a common death for a common faith." (Bruce)

2. (12-17) Life of the new man.

Therefore, as *the* elect of God, holy and beloved, put on tender mercies, kindness, humility, meekness, longsuffering; bearing with one another, and forgiving one another, if anyone has a complaint against another; even as Christ forgave you, so you also *must do*. But above all these things put on love, which is the bond of perfection. And let the peace of God rule in your hearts, to which also you were called in one body; and be thankful. Let the word of Christ dwell in you richly in all wisdom, teaching and admonishing one another in psalms and hymns and spiritual songs, singing with grace in your hearts to the Lord. And *whatever* you do in word or deed, *do* all in the name of the Lord Jesus, giving thanks to God the Father through Him.

a. **Therefore, as the elect of God**: The new man is **elect of God**. This means that God has *chosen* the Christian, and chosen him to be something special in His plan. "**Elect**" is a word that frightens some, but it should be taken both as a comfort and as a destiny to fulfill.

b. **Put on tender mercies, kindness, humility**: Each one of the qualities mentioned in this passage express themselves in *relationships*. A significant measure of our Christian life is found simply in how we treat people and the quality of our relationships with them.

i. "It is most significant to note that every one of the graces listed has to do with personal relationships between man and man. There is no mention of virtues like efficiency or cleverness, not even of diligence or industry – not that these things are unimportant. But the great basic Christian virtues are those which govern human relationships." (Barclay)

ii. **Tender mercies**: If something is **tender**, it is sensitive to touch. "The apostle would have them to *feel* the *slightest touch* of another's misery; and, as their clothes are put over their body, so their tenderest feeling should be always within reach of the miserable." (Clarke)

iii. **Kindness**: "The ancient writers defined *chrestotes* as the virtue of the man whose neighbour's good is as dear to him as his own.... It is used of wine which has grown mellow with age and lost its harshness. It is the word used when Jesus said, 'My yoke is *easy*.' (Matthew 11:30)." (Barclay)

iv. We can say that **humility** (which was *not* considered a virtue among the ancient Greeks) is the "parent" of both **meekness** and **longsuffering**. **Meekness** shows how **humility** will effect my *actions* towards others; I will not dominate, manipulate, or coerce for my own ends, even if I have the power and the ability. **Longsuffering** shows how **humility** will effect my *reaction* towards others; I will not become impatient, short, or filled with resentment towards the weaknesses and sins of others.

c. **Forgiving one another, if anyone has a complaint against another; even as Christ forgave you, so you also must do**: We are told to live **forgiving one another**, after the pattern of Jesus' forgiveness towards us. Understanding the way Jesus forgave us will always make us *more* generous with forgiveness, and never less generous.

i. When we consider the staggering debt Jesus forgave for us, and the comparative smallness of the debts others have toward us, it is base ingratitude for us to not forgive them (as in the parable Jesus spoke in Matthew 18:21-35). "The forgiveness they have received is used to enforce the duty of forgiving others." (Peake)

ii. When one thinks of how **Christ forgave you** it should make us much more generous with forgiveness.

- God holds back His anger a very long time when we sin against Him. He bears with us a long time, even when we sorely provoke Him.

- God reaches out to *bad people* to bring forgiveness to them; the habit of man is to not reconcile if the offending person is a person of bad character.

- God makes the first move towards us in forgiveness; the habit of man is to only be reconciled if the offending party craves forgiveness and makes the first move.

- God forgives often knowing that we will sin again, sometimes in the exact same way. It is the habit of man to forgive only if the offending party solemnly promises to never do the wrong again.

- God's forgiveness is so complete and glorious that He grants adoption to those former offenders. In the habit of man, even when forgiveness is offered, he will not lift again the former offender to a place of high status and partnership.

- God bore *all* the penalty for the wrong we did against Him. In the habit of man, when he is wronged, he will not forgive unless the offender agrees to bear all the penalty for the wrong done.

- God keeps reaching out to man for reconciliation even when man refuses Him again and again. In the habit of man, one will not continue to offer reconciliation if it is rejected once.

- God requires no probationary period to receive His forgiveness; in the habit of man, one will not restore an offender without a period of probation.

- God's forgiveness offers complete restoration and honor; in the habit of man, we feel we should be complimented when we merely *tolerate* those who sin against us.

- Once having forgiven, God puts His trust in us and invites us back to work with Him as co-laborers. In the habit of man, one will not trust someone who has formerly wronged him.

iii. "Suppose that someone had grievously offended any one of you, and that he asked your forgiveness, do you not think that you would probably say to him, 'Well, yes, I forgive you; but I - I - I - cannot forget it'? Ah! dear friends, that is a sort of forgiveness with one leg chopped off, it is a lame forgiveness, and is not worth much." (Spurgeon)

d. **Above all these things put on love, which is the bond of perfection**: **Love** is the summary of all the things described in this passage. Love perfectly fulfills what God requires of us in relationships.

i. **But above all these things put on love**: "*Upon all, over all*; as the *outer garment* envelopes all the clothing, so let *charity* or *love* invest and encompass all the rest... Let this, therefore, be as the *upper garment*... that invests the whole man." (Clarke)

ii. "All the virtues listed in vv. 12, 13 are, on the highest level, manifestations of love; but love is larger than any one of them, indeed, larger than all of them combined." (Vaughan)

iii. "The other virtues, pursued without love, become distorted and unbalanced." (Wright)

e. **And let the peace of God rule in your hearts, to which also you were called in one body**: The rule of **the peace of God** means that **peace** should *characterize* the community of God's people, and that **peace** is a standard for discerning God's will.

i. "The apostle says, Let it rule. The Greek word means arbitrate. Whenever there is a doubtful issue to be decided, and by one course your peace may be disturbed, whilst by another it may be maintained, choose the things that make for peace, whether for yourselves or others. Let God's peace act as umpire." (Meyer)

ii. "Let the peace of Christ *judge, decide*, and *govern* in your hearts, as the *brabeus*, or judge, does in the Olympic contests.... When a man loses his *peace*, it is an awful proof that he has lost something else that he has given way to evil, and grieved the Spirit of God." (Clarke)

iii. Wright sees the context of community: "'Peace' here is not the inward, individual peace of mind which accompanies humble confident trust in God's love, but a peace which characterizes the community, the 'body' as a whole."

f. **Let the word of Christ dwell in you richly in all wisdom, teaching and admonishing one another in psalms and hymns and spiritual songs**: The new man walks in the word of God and in worship with other believers.

i. **Dwell in you**: "There appears to be here an allusion to the *Shechinah*, or symbol of the Divine presence, which *dwelt* in the *tabernacle* and first *temple*." (Clarke)

ii. **Psalms and hymns and spiritual songs**: This variety suggests that God delights in creative, spontaneous worship. The emphasis is more on *variety* than on *strict categories*. "We can scarcely say what is the exact difference between these three expressions." (Clarke)

iii. "The word of Christ is to dwell in them so richly that it finds spontaneous expression in religious song in the Christian assemblies or the home." (Peake)

g. **Do all in the name of the Lord Jesus**: The new man lives his life, **all** his life, for Jesus. He will only seek to do the things that he *may* do **in the name of the Lord Jesus**, and he will persevere in the difficulty of doing such things, knowing that he is doing them **in the name of the Lord Jesus**.

3. (18-19) The new man's marriage relationship.

Wives, submit to your own husbands, as is fitting in the Lord. Husbands, love your wives and do not be bitter toward them.

a. **Wives, submit**: The ancient Greek word translated **submit** is essentially a word borrowed from the military. It literally means "to be under in rank." It speaks of the way that an army is organized among levels of rank, with generals and colonels and majors and captains and sergeants and privates. There are levels of rank, and one is obligated to respect those in higher rank.

i. We know that as a person, a private can be smarter, more talented, and be a better person than a general. But he is still *under rank* to the general. He isn't submitted to the general so much as a *person* as he is to the general as a *general*. In the same way, the wife doesn't submit to her husband because he *deserves* it. She submits because he is her husband.

ii. The idea of submission doesn't have anything to do with someone being smarter or better or more talented. It has to do with a God-appointed order. "Anyone who has served in the armed forces knows that 'rank' has to do with order and authority, not with value or ability." (Wiersbe)

iii. "The equality of men and women before the Lord, of which Paul wrote in Galatians 3:28, has not been retracted: but neither does it mean identity of role or function." (Wright)

iv. Therefore, submission means you are part of a team. If the family is a team, then the husband is "captain" of the team. The wife has her place in relation to the "captain," and the children have their place in relation to the "captain" and the wife.

v. "The form of the verb (*hypotassesthe*, middle voice) shows that the submission is to be voluntary. The wife's submission is never to be forced on her by a demanding husband; it is the deference that a loving wife, conscious that her home (just as any other institution) must have a head, gladly shows." (Vaughan)

b. **Wives, submit to your own husbands**: This defines the *sphere* of a wife's submission - to her **own husband**. The Bible never commands nor recommends a *general* submission of women unto men. It is commanded only in the spheres of the home and in the church. God does not command that men have exclusive authority in the areas of politics, business, education, and so on.

c. **As is fitting in the Lord**: This is a crucial phrase. It colors everything else we understand about this passage. There have been two main "wrong" interpretations of this phrase, each favoring a certain "position."

i. The interpretation that "favors" the husband says that **as is fitting in the Lord** means that a wife should submit to her husband as if he were God himself. The idea is "you submit to God in absolutely everything without question, so you must submit to your husband in the same absolute way." This thinks that **as is fitting in the Lord** defines the *extent* of submission. But this is wrong. Simply put, *in no place* does the Scripture say that a person should submit to another in that way. There are limits to the submission your employer can expect of you. There are limits to the submission the government can expect of you. There are limits to the submission parents can expect of children. In no place does the Scripture teach an unqualified, without exception, submission – except to God and God alone. To violate this is to commit the sin of idolatry.

ii. The interpretation that "favors" the wife says that **as is fitting in the Lord** means "I'll submit to him as long as he does what the Lord wants." And then it is the wife's job to decide what the Lord wants. This thinks that **as is fitting in the Lord** defines the *limit* of submission. This is also wrong. It is true that there are limits to a wife's submission, but when the wife approaches **as is fitting in the Lord** in this way, then it degenerates into a case of "I'll submit to my husband when I agree with him. I'll submit to him when he makes the right decisions and carries them out the right way. When he makes a wrong decision, he isn't **in the Lord**, so I shouldn't submit to him then. It isn't **fitting** to do so." Simply put, *that is not submission at all.* Except for those who are just plain cantankerous and argumentative, *everyone* submits to others when they are in agreement. It is only when there is a *disagreement* that submission is tested.

iii. **As is fitting in the Lord** does not define the *extent* of a wife's submission. It does not define the *limit* of a wife's submission. It defines the *motive* of a wife's submission. It means, "Wives, submit yourselves unto your own husbands because it is a part of your duty to the Lord, because it is an expression of your submission to the Lord." They submit simply because it **is fitting in the Lord** to do it. It honors God's Word and His order of authority. It is part of their Christian duty and discipleship.

iv. "The phrase 'in the Lord' indicates that wifely submission is proper not only in the natural order but also in the Christian order. The whole thing, then, is lifted to a new and higher level." (Vaughan)

v. Therefore, **as is fitting in the Lord** means:

- For wives, submission to their husband is part of their Christian life.

- When a wife doesn't obey this word to **submit to your own husband as is fitting in the Lord**, she doesn't just fall short as a wife. She falls short as a follower of Jesus Christ.

- This means that the command to submit is completely out of the realm of "my nature" or "my personality." Wives aren't expected to submit because they are the "submissive type." They are expected to submit because it is **fitting in the Lord.**

- This has nothing to do with your husband's intelligence or giftedness or capability. It has to do with honoring the Lord Jesus Christ.

- This has nothing to do with whether or not your husband is "right" on a particular issue. It has to do with Jesus being right.

- This means that a woman should take great care in how she *chooses* her husband. Remember, ladies: this is what God requires of you in marriage. This is *His* expectation of you. Instead of looking for an attractive man, instead of looking for a wealthy man, instead of looking for a romantic man, you better first look for a man you can *respect*.

vi. As is the case in every human relationship, the command to submit is not absolute. There are exceptions to this command for a wife to **submit to her own husband**.

- When the husband asks the wife to sin, she must not submit.

- When the husband is medically incapacitated, insane, or under the influence of mind altering substances, the wife may not submit.

- When the husband is violent and physically threatening, the wife may not submit.

- When the husband breaks the marriage bond by adultery, the wife does not need to submit to her husband being in an adulterous relationship.

vii. "If a Stoic disciple asked why he should behave in a particular way, his teacher would no doubt tell him that it was 'fitting' because it was in conformity with nature. When a Christian convert asked the same question, he was told that such behavior was 'fitting in the Lord'; members of the believing community should live thus for Christ's sake." (Bruce)

d. **Husbands, love your wives**: Paul's words to husbands safeguards his words to wives. Though wives are to submit to their husbands, it never excuses husbands acting as tyrants over their wives. Instead, a husband must **love** his wife, and the ancient Greek word translated **love** here is *agape*.

i. Significantly, this puts an obligation upon the **husbands**. In the ancient world – under Jewish, Greek, and Roman customs, *all* power and privileges belonged to husbands in regard to wives, to fathers in regard to children, and to masters in regard to slaves. There were no complimentary powers or privileges on the part of wives, children, or slaves.

ii. "*Agapao* does not denote affection or romantic attachment; it rather denotes caring love, a deliberate attitude of mind that concerns itself with the well-being of the one loved." (Vaughan)

iii. Strictly speaking, *agape* can't be defined as "God's love," because men are said to *agape* sin and the world (John 3:19, 1 John 2:15). But it can be defined as a sacrificial, giving, absorbing, love. The word has little to do with emotion; it has much to do with self-denial for the sake of another.

- It is a love that loves without changing.

- It is a self-giving love that gives without demanding or expecting re-payment.

- It is love so great that it can be given to the unlovable or unappealing.

- It is love that loves even when it is rejected.

- *Agape* love gives and loves because it wants to; it does not demand or expect repayment from the love given. It gives because it loves, it does not love in order to receive.

iv. We can read this passage and think that Paul means, "Husband, be kind to your wife." Or "Husband, be nice to your wife." There is no doubt that for many marriages, this would be a huge improvement. But that isn't what Paul writes about. What he really means is, "Husband, continually practice self-denial for the sake of your wife."

v. Of course, this *agape* love is the kind of love Jesus has for His people and this is the love husbands should imitate towards their wives (Ephesians 5:25).

e. **And do not be bitter toward them**: The implication is perhaps the wife has given the husband some *reason* **to be bitter**. Paul says, "That doesn't matter, husband." The husband may feel perfectly justified in his harsh or unloving attitude and actions towards his wife, but he is not justified - *no matter how the wife has been towards the husband.*

i. *Agape* loves even when there are obvious and glaring deficiencies, even when the receiver is unworthy of the love.

4. (20-21) The new man's parent and child relationship.

Children, obey your parents in all things, for this is well pleasing to the Lord. Fathers, do not provoke your children, lest they become discouraged.

a. **Children, obey your parents in all things**: Paul has in mind children who are still in their parents' household and under their authority. For these, they must not only *honor* their father and mother (as in Ephesians 6:2), but they must also **obey** them, and **obey** them **in all things**.

i. When a child is grown and out of his parents' household, he is no longer under the same obligation of *obedience*, but the obligation to *honor your father and mother* remains.

b. **For this is well pleasing to the Lord**: This is one of the important *reasons* for a child's obedience. When a child respects his parent's authority, he is respecting God's order of authority in other areas of life.

i. This idea of an order of authority and submission to an order of authority are so important to God that they are part of His very being. The First Person of the Holy Trinity is called the *Father*; the Second Person of the Holy Trinity is called the *Son*. Inherent in those titles is a relationship of authority and submission to authority.

ii. The Father exercises authority over the Son, and the Son submits to the Father's authority - and this is in the very nature and being of God! Our failure to exercise Biblical authority, and our failure to submit to Biblical authority, isn't just wrong and sad - it sins against the very nature of God. Remember 1 Samuel 15:23: *For rebellion is as the sin of witchcraft.*

c. **Fathers, do not provoke your children**: Children have a responsibility to obey, but parents - here, put into one as **fathers** - have a responsibility to **not provoke** their **children**. Parents can **provoke** their children by being too harsh, too demanding, too controlling, unforgiving, or just plain angry. This harshness can be expressed through words, through actions, or through non-verbal communication.

i. In most parenting problems, the parent blames the child. It is easy to do because the problem is usually most evident in the bad behavior in the child. But Paul wisely reminds us that the bad behavior may actually be *provoked* by the parent. When this is the case, it doesn't justify the bad behavior of the child, but it may explain part of its cause. It is commanded of parents to do everything they can to **not provoke** their **children**.

ii. **Provoke**: "Irritate by exacting commands and perpetual faultfinding and interference for interference' sake." (Peake)

iii. "Parents, and specially fathers, are urged not to irritate their children by being so unreasonable in their demands that their children lose heart and come to think that it is useless trying to please their parents." (Bruce)

iv. "The word 'fathers' can refer to parents of both sexes, though it may well have an eye to the importance of the father's role, within God's created order, in the upbringing of children." (Wright)

d. **Lest they become discouraged**: Children who grow up with parents who provoke them will **become discouraged**. They will not feel the love and the support from their parents like they should, and they will come to believe that the whole world is against them because they feel their parents are against them. This reminds us how important it is to season our parenting with lots of grace. Perhaps we should be as gracious, gentle, forgiving, and longsuffering with our children as God is with us.

5. (3:22-4:1) The new man's servant and master relationship.

Bondservants, obey in all things your masters according to the flesh, not with eyeservice, as men-pleasers, but in sincerity of heart, fearing God. And whatever you do, do it heartily, as to the Lord and not to men, knowing that from the Lord you will receive the reward of the inheritance; for you serve the Lord Christ. But he who does wrong will be repaid for what he has done, and there is no partiality. Masters, give your bondservants what is just and fair, knowing that you also have a Master in heaven.

a. **Obey in all things your masters according to the flesh**: As Christians put on the new man, they will show a properly submissive attitude towards their **masters** - in a modern context, towards their employer or supervisor.

i. This is another sphere of God's order of authority. Employees have a God-ordained role of obedience and submission to their employers or supervisors.

ii. "It will be noted that this section is far longer than the other two; and its length may well be due to long talks which Paul had with the runaway slave, Onesimus, whom later he was to send back to his master Philemon." (Barclay)

iii. "More than half the people seen on the streets of the great cities of the Roman world were slaves. And this was the status of the majority of 'professional' people such as teachers and doctors as well as that of menials and craftsmen." (Vaughan)

b. **Not with eyeservice, as men-pleasers, but in sincerity of heart, fearing God**: We are always tempted to work just as hard as we have to, thinking we only have to please man. But God wants every worker to see that ultimately, they work for *Him*. Therefore, they should **do it heartily,**

as to the Lord and not to men. God promises to **reward** those who work with that kind of heart.

i. The Christian who is a dishonest, lazy or unreliable worker has something far worse to deal with than a reprimand from his earthly supervisor. His heavenly supervisor may prepare a reprimand as well.

ii. "Far more culpable is the attitude of modern 'clockwatchers,' who have contracted to serve their employer and receive an agreed remuneration for their labor. But Christian slaves – or Christian employees today – have the highest of all motives for faithful and conscientious performance of duty; they are above all else servants of Christ, and will work first and foremost so as to please him." (Bruce)

iii. **The reward of the inheritance**: "One should properly read '*the* inheritance'; the reference is clearly to the life of the age to come. This is ironic, since in earthly terms slaves could not inherit property." (Wright)

iv. **For you serve the Lord Christ**: "The force of this unusual phrase (Paul nowhere else allows the titles 'Lord' and 'Christ' to stand together without the name 'Jesus' as well) could be brought out by a paraphrase: 'so work for the true Master – Christ!'" (Wright)

c. **But he who does wrong will be repaid for what he has done**: When a Christian worker does poorly in his job, he should not expect special leniency from his boss, especially if his boss is a Christian. Being a Christian should make us *more* responsible, not *less* responsible.

i. "It is possible for an unfaithful servant to wrong and defraud his master in a great variety of ways without being detected; but let all such remember what is here said: he that doeth wrong shall receive for the wrong which he has done; God sees him, and will punish him for his breach of honesty and trust." (Clarke)

ii. **Will be repaid... and there is no partiality**: For ancient Christian slaves and for modern Christian workers, there is no guarantee on earth of fairness of treatment from those whom they work for. Sometimes **partiality** means that bad workers are unfairly rewarded and good employees are penalized or left unrewarded. Paul assures both our ancient brethren and us that there is a final rewarding and punishment, and with this **there is no partiality**.

iii. In Ephesians 6:9 Paul addressed masters and warned *them* that there was *no partiality with* God. Here, he warned *servants* that there is **no partiality** with God. "In Ephesians masters are not to think that God is influenced by social position; in the present passage, slaves are not to act unscrupulously just because they know men treat them as irresponsible chattel." (Vaughan)

d. **Masters, give your bondservants what is just and fair**: As Christians put on the new man, they will be **just and fair** to those who work for them. It is a terrible thing for a boss to cheat or mistreat his workers, but far worse for a Christian to do it.

i. **Just and fair**: This is even more powerful than a command for masters to be *kind* or *pleasant* to slaves. One can be kind or pleasant to animals or pets; but we are only **just and fair** to fellow human beings. Paul asked masters to make a recognition that would undermine the very foundations of slavery.

ii. Through the history of Christianity, there have been some who used these passages where Paul speaks to slaves and their masters to *justify* or even *promote* the practice of slavery. Others have *blamed* these passages for the practice of slavery. Yet one can never blame Christianity for slavery; it was a universal practice that pre-dated both Christianity and the Jewish nation. Instead, one should see that the *abolition* of slavery came from Christian people and impulses, and not from any other major religion and certainly not from secularism.

iii. Without making an overt protest against slavery, Paul seemed to understand that if he could establish the point that slaves were equals in the body of Christ, full human beings with both responsibilities and rights (that they should be treated in a manner both **just and fair**), then in time the whole structure of slavery in the Roman Empire would crumble – and it did.

Colossians 4 - Prayer Life, Personal Witness, and Final Greetings

A. The inner life of prayer and the outer life of witness.

1. (2-4) The inner life of prayer.

Continue earnestly in prayer, being vigilant in it with thanksgiving; meanwhile praying also for us, that God would open to us a door for the word, to speak the mystery of Christ, for which I am also in chains, that I may make it manifest, as I ought to speak.

a. **Continue earnestly in prayer**: Paul supported the Colossian church through His prayers for them (Colossians 1:3-8). Their life and ministry would continue to prosper through continued vigilance in prayer, including prayer on their part.

   i. The ancient Greek word translated **continue** is "Built on a root meaning 'to be strong,' it always connotes earnest adherence to a person or thing. In this passage it implies persistence and fervor." (Vaughan)

   ii. This sort of *earnest* prayer is important, but does not come easy. **Earnestly in prayer** speaks of great effort steadily applied. "Heaven's gate is not to be stormed by one weapon but by many. Spare no arrows, Christian. Watch and see that none of the arms in thy armoury are rusty. Besiege the throne of God with a hundred hands, and look at the promise with a hundred eyes. You have a great work on hand for you have to move the arm that moves the world; watch, then, for every means of moving that arm. See to it that you ply every promise; that you use every argument; that you wrestle with all might." (Spurgeon)

b. **Being vigilant in it with thanksgiving**: We are to be **vigilant** in prayer, but always praying **with thanksgiving** for the great things God has done.

   i. Barclay on **vigilant**: "Literally the Greek means to be *wakeful*. The phrase could well mean that Paul is telling them not to go to sleep

116

when they pray." Sometimes, because of the tiredness of our body or mind, we struggle against sleep when we pray. Or, we pray *as if* we were asleep, and our prayers simply sound and feel tired and sleepy.

ii. "Prayer should be mingled with praise. I have heard that in New England after the Puritans had settled there a long while, they used to have very often a day of humiliation, fasting, and prayer, till they had so many days of fasting, humiliation, and prayer, that at last a good senator proposed that they should change it for once, and have a day of thanksgiving." (Spurgeon)

iii. "The connection here with thanksgiving may suggest the threefold rhythm: intercession, 'watching' for answers to prayer, and thanksgiving when answers appear." (Wright)

c. **Meanwhile praying also for us**: Paul seemed to say, "As long as we are on the subject of prayer, please pray **for us**!" But Paul didn't ask for prayer for his personal needs (which were many), but **that God would open to us a door for the word**.

i. The same word picture of an open door as an open opportunity for the gospel is seen in passages such as Acts 14:27, 1 Corinthians 16:9, and 2 Corinthians 2:12.

d. **As I ought to speak**: Even though Paul was **in chains** for his faithfulness to the gospel, he knew that he **ought to speak** it in a way that would **make it manifest** (clearly evident). Paul wanted prayer that he would continue to make the gospel clear and evident, even if it meant more **chains**.

i. Robertson comments on Paul's words, **as I ought to speak**: "Wonderful as Paul's preaching was to his hearers and seems to us, he was never satisfied with it. What preacher can be?"

2. (5-6) The outer life of witness.

Walk in wisdom toward those *who are* outside, redeeming the time. *Let* your speech always *be* with grace, seasoned with salt, that you may know how you ought to answer each one.

a. **Walk in wisdom toward those who are outside**: The Christian life isn't only lived in the prayer closet. There also must be practical, lived-out Christianity, living wisely **toward those who are outside**. How we *speak* has a lot to do with this, so we must let our **speech always be with grace**.

i. "Distorted accounts of Christian conduct and belief were in circulation; it was important that Christians should give no color to these calumnies, but should rather give the lie to them by their regular manner of life." (Bruce)

ii. **Let your speech always be with grace**: "The word 'grace' has, in Greek as in English, the possible double meaning of God's grace and human graciousness." (Wright)

iii. "In classical writers 'salt' expressed the wit with which conversation was flavoured." (Peake) "Grace and salt (wit, sense) make an ideal combination." (Robertson)

b. **That you may know how you ought to answer each one**: Paul believed that Christians would **answer** others from Biblical truth, and that they would work at knowing how to communicate those answers to **those who are outside**.

i. Barclay translates Colossians 4:6 this way: *Let your speech always be with gracious charm, seasoned with the salt of wit, so that you will know the right answer to give in every case.* He explains: "The Christian must commend his message with the charm and the wit which were in Jesus himself."

ii. "They must strive to cultivate the gift of pleasant and wise conversation, so that they may be able to speak appropriately to each individual (with his peculiar needs)." (Peake)

iii. Colossians 4:2-6 shows that God is concerned *both* about our personal prayer life *and* our interaction with the world. He cares both about the prayer closet and the public street, and He wants us to care about both also.

iv. This is an important idea to connect with earlier passages of Colossians. Paul spent much time in this letter explaining the truth and refuting bad doctrine. Yet all the correct knowledge was of little good until it was applied in *both* the prayer closet and the public street of daily life. We could say that here, Paul genuinely completes his letter.

B. Personal notes concluding the letter.

1. (7-9) Regarding Tychicus and Onesimus, messengers of the letter.

Tychicus, a beloved brother, faithful minister, and fellow servant in the Lord, will tell you all the news about me. I am sending him to you for this very purpose, that he may know your circumstances and comfort your hearts, with Onesimus, a faithful and beloved brother, who is *one* of you. They will make known to you all things which *are happening* here.

a. **Tychicus, a beloved brother**: Apparently, the Colossian Christians didn't know who Tychicus was. He would carry this letter to them (**will tell you all the news about me**).

i. Apparently Epaphras, who brought the news from Colosse to Paul in Rome (Colossians 1:7), would not return to Colosse soon; so Paul sent **Tychicus** instead.

ii. **Tychicus** is noted in Acts 20:4 as one of the men who came with Paul from the Roman province of Asia to Jerusalem, to carry the offering of those believers to the needy Christians of Jerusalem and Judea.

iii. "The reference to Tychicus is almost word for word identical with Ephesians 6:21-22. He was evidently the bearer of the letter to the Ephesians as well as this one." (Bruce)

b. **With Onesimus, a faithful and beloved brother**: Onesimus was a slave owned by a believer in Colosse, but he ran away and came into contact with Paul in Rome. There, Onesimus became a Christian and a dedicated helper to Paul. His story is continued in Paul's letter to Philemon.

i. Paul *could have* wrote about Onesimus, "the escaped slave who I am sending back to his master." Instead, he called him **a faithful and beloved brother**, and let the Colossian Christians know that Onesimus was now **one of you**.

2. (10-11) Greetings from three of Paul's faithful Jewish friends.

Aristarchus my fellow prisoner greets you, with Mark the cousin of Barnabas (about whom you received instructions: if he comes to you, welcome him), and Jesus who is called Justus. These *are my* only fellow workers for the kingdom of God who are of the circumcision; they have proved to be a comfort to me.

a. **Aristarchus**: He was a Macedonian from Thessalonica (Acts 20:4). He was Paul's travel companion, and with the apostle when the Ephesian mob seized Paul (Acts 19:29). He was also with Paul when he set sail for Rome under his Roman imprisonment (Acts 27:2). Here Paul calls him **my fellow prisoner**. It seems that **Aristarchus** had an interesting habit of being *with* Paul in hard times. Some (such as William Ramsay) suggest that he actually made himself Paul's slave so that he could travel with him on this journey to Rome.

b. **Mark the cousin of Barnabas... if he comes to you, welcome him**: Though Paul had much earlier a falling out with both Barnabas and Mark (Acts 13:5, 13:13, and 15:36-40), clearly by the time he wrote this all was in the past. The grace of God working in Paul meant that time changed him and softened him towards others who had previously offended him.

i. "It is from this reference alone that we learn that Mark was Barnabas' cousin – a piece of information which throws light on the special consideration which Barnabas gives to Mark in Acts." (Bruce)

ii. Because Paul identified Mark in terms of his relationships with Barnabas, it seems that the Colossian Christians knew who Barnabas was. Either this was through his reputation or through further missionary journeys that were not recorded in the Book of Acts. It reminds us that the Book of Acts is an *incomplete* record of the history of the early church.

c. **Jesus who is called Justus**: Of this man, we know nothing except his name. He is numbered among these previous four men, all of them *comforters* to Paul in his Roman custody preceding his trial before Caesar (**they have proved to be a comfort to me**).

d. **My only fellow workers... who are of the circumcision**: At that time, Paul had only three **fellow workers** with a Jewish heritage. Yet these three did a great work, they **proved to be a comfort to** Paul.

i. Paul was in Roman custody because of a Jewish riot on the temple mount over the mere mention of God's offer of grace to the Gentiles (Acts 22:21-22).

ii. Adam Clarke drew out a logical conclusion from the words, **These are my only fellow workers for the kingdom of God who are of the circumcision**: "It is evident, therefore, that Peter was not now at Rome, else he certainly would have been mentioned in this list... indeed, there is no evidence that Peter ever saw Rome."

3. (12-13) Greetings from Epaphras.

Epaphras, who is *one* of you, a bondservant of Christ, greets you, always laboring fervently for you in prayers, that you may stand perfect and complete in all the will of God. For I bear him witness that he has a great zeal for you, and those who are in Laodicea, and those in Hierapolis.

a. **Always laboring fervently for you in prayers**: Prayer is hard work, and Epaphras worked diligently at it, especially knowing the danger of the false teaching in Colosse. So, Epaphras prayed that the Colossian Christians would **stand perfect and complete in all the will of God**. This is a wonderful prayer to pray for anyone.

i. Paul called Epaphras a **bondservant of Christ**, using a phrase that he often applied to himself, but never to anyone else, except here and in Philippians 1:1 where he speaks of himself and Timothy together as *bondservants* of Jesus.

ii. Epaphras was a **bondservant**, and *prayer* was an important area where he worked hard. **Laboring fervently** "is a free translation of *echei polyn ponon*, a phrase the key word of which (*ponom*) suggest heavy toil to the extent of pain." (Vaughan)

b. **He has a great zeal for you**: Epaphras prayed well because he *cared* well. If he lagged in **zeal**, he certainly would have lagged in prayer.

4. (14) Greetings from Luke and Demas.

Luke the beloved physician and Demas greet you.

a. **Luke the beloved physician**: This is the one passage that informs us that Luke, the human author of the Gospel of Luke and the Book of Acts, was a physician. We also see that his works are written with a more scientific, analytical mindset (Luke 1:1-4) and have much detail that a physician would be interested in (Luke 4:38, 5:12-15, and 8:43).

i. Perhaps Luke was in Rome to deliver a document he recently finished - the *Gospel of Luke* and the *Book of Acts*, which probably were together a "friend of the court" report, explaining to the Romans why Paul stood before Caesar's court.

b. **Demas**: Here, nothing positive is said about **Demas**, only that he greets the Colossian Christians and therefore must have been known to them. In Philemon 1:24 he is grouped among Paul's *fellow laborers*. Yet in the last mention of him (2 Timothy 4:10), Paul said that Demas had forsaken him, *having loved this present world*, and that he had gone on to Thessalonica.

i. "Surely here we have the faint outlines of a study in degeneration, loss of enthusiasm and failure in the faith." (Barclay)

ii. The six people who greeted the Colossians were connected with Paul in Rome, during the custody before appearing on trial before Caesar. This shows that during this imprisonment – unlike the later one described in 2 Timothy – Paul, though chained, enjoyed at least the occasional company of many friends and associates.

5. (15) Greeting to Nymphas and the Laodiceans.

Greet the brethren who are in Laodicea, and Nymphas and the church that *is* in his house.

a. **Laodicea**: This was the same city later mentioned in the scathing rebuke of Revelation 3:14-22, and it was a neighboring city of Colosse, along with Hierapolis (Colossians 4:13).

b. **Nymphas**: There has been some considerable debate as to if Paul referred to a *man* or a *woman* with this name. Some manuscripts have the masculine form and some have the feminine.

i. "Much ink has been spilt over the question whether the individual here mentioned is a woman (Nympha) or a man (Nymphas). Both forms are found in the manuscript tradition, and certainty seems impossible on this (fortunately not very significant) point." (Wright)

c. **Church that is in his house**: With no buildings of their own, the early church met as "house churches." Because few houses were large, there were usually several house churches in a city, with a pastor or elder over each.

i. "Such house-churches were apparently smaller circles of fellowship within the larger fellowship of the city *ekklesia*." (Bruce)

ii. "We must remember that there was no such thing as a special Church building until the third century. Up to that time the Christian congregations met in the houses of those who where the leaders of the Church." (Barclay)

6. (16) Instructions for spreading the message in this letter.

Now when this epistle is read among you, see that it is read also in the church of the Laodiceans, and that you likewise read the epistle from Laodicea.

a. **Now when this epistle is read among you**: When Paul and other apostles wrote letters to churches, the letters were simply publicly read in the congregations. It was a way for the apostle to teach that church even when he could not personally be there.

b. **See that it is read also in the church of the Laodiceans**: It was the general practice to distribute all apostolic letters among the churches, especially those close to each other.

i. "Here we undoubtedly have the principle reason for the preservation of Paul's letters in the sub-apostolic period, and their eventual adoption as part of the canonical 'new covenant' books: their author intended them to carry, in writing, the authority which had been invested in him as an apostle." (Wright)

ii. This helps us to understand how and why the letters would have been copied almost immediately, and how slight mistakes in copying the manuscripts could come in at an early date.

c. **And that you likewise read the epistle from Laodicea**: Apparently, Paul wrote a letter to the Laodiceans that we do not have. We should not assume from this that our Bible is incomplete. The Holy Spirit has chosen to preserve those letters that are inspired for the church in a universal sense. Paul was not inspired in this way every time he set pen to paper.

i. It may be that this "missing" Laodicean letter was actually the letter to the Ephesians. "It is well-nigh certain that *Ephesians* was not written to the Church at Ephesus but was an encyclical letter meant to circulate among the Churches of Asia. It may be that this encyclical had reached Laodicea and was now on the way to Colosse." (Barclay)

ii. There is a Latin letter of Paul to the Laodiceans and it was mentioned as early as the fifth century by Jerome. But Jerome himself called it a forgery and that most people in his day agreed that it was not authentic. It is mainly made up of phrases from Philippians and Galatians. Adam Clarke had a low opinion of this letter: "As to its being the work of St. Paul, little or nothing need be said; its barrenness of meaning, poverty of style, incoherency of manner, and total want of design and object, are a sufficient refutation of its pretensions."

7. (17) A special word to Archippus.

And say to Archippus, "Take heed to the ministry which you have received in the Lord, that you may fulfill it."

a. **And say to Archippus**: This special word to **Archippus** is of special interest. Paul wrote another short word regarding **Archippus** in another letter, mentioning *Archippus our fellow soldier, and to the church in your house* (Philemon 1:2).

i. This mention in Philemon 1:2 makes some people believe that he was the son of Philemon, since he is mentioned in the context of the wife of Philemon (*Apphia*) and his household (*the church in your house*). It also shows that Paul thought highly of Archippus and valued him as an associate in God's work (*our fellow soldier*).

ii. The context of Colossians 4:17 leads some to think that though Archippus was part of the family of Philemon, he was connected with the church at Laodicea. Perhaps Archippus was the pastor of the church at Laodicea. Of course, there is no way to know this for certain.

b. **Say to Archippus, "Take heed to the ministry"**: Paul wanted Archippus to be encouraged and strengthened, but he did not make this appeal to Archippus directly. He asked that it come to Archippus *through* the Colossians (or the Laodiceans).

i. "Presumably he would be present when the letter was read, either in the Colossian church or, later, when it had been sent to Laodicea. This was perhaps calculated to impress him the more with the solemnity of his responsibility to carry out his service." (Bruce)

ii. Therefore, it was *more fitting* for the Colossians (or Laodiceans) to say this to Archippus than for Paul himself to say it to him. He needed to hear this from the people around him: "Fulfill your ministry." When the Colossians spoke up, then Archippus knew his ministry was *wanted*. "Many an *Archippus* is sluggish, because the *Colossians* are silent." (Dyke)

iii. They need to say *"fulfill your ministry"* directly *to* Archippus, not *behind* him. Whispering it behind his back would do no good. They had to say it *to* him.

c. **Take heed to the ministry**: This encouragement to **Archippus** spoke both to him and to us regarding some enduring principles of ministry.

- God gives **ministry** to His people.

- True **ministry** is **received in the Lord**.

- **Ministry** *may* be left *unfulfilled*.

- One must **take heed** to their ministry in order for it to be **fulfilled**.

- We should encourage *others* to **fulfill** their **ministry**.

  i. "It is more likely, therefore, that the words of the apostle convey no censure, but are rather intended to stir him up to further diligence, and to encourage him in the work, seeing he had so much false doctrine and so many false teachers to contend with." (Clarke)

  ii. Thinking Archippus to be a pastor, Trapp applied the principle of **take heed to the ministry** to him: "The Church is thy proper element, the pulpit thy right *ubi* [place]; the sanctuary should be the centre of all thy circumference."

8. (18) Conclusion.

This salutation by my own hand—Paul. Remember my chains. Grace *be* with you. Amen.

a. **This salutation by my own hand**: As was the custom in that day, Paul generally dictated his letters and personally signed a postscript with his **own hand**.

b. **Remember my chains**: There is much emotion, sorrow, and strength in this simple phrase. Paul not only knew the confinement and loneliness of the prisoner; he also had the uncertainty of not knowing if his case before Caesar's court would end with his execution.

  i. "The chain clanked afresh as Paul took the pen to sign the salutation. He was not likely to forget it himself." (Robertson)

  ii. "Paul's references to his sufferings are not pleas for sympathy; they are his claims to authority, the guarantees of his right to speak." (Barclay)

c. **Grace be with you**: Paul's conclusion is the only one possible for the apostle of grace, confronting a heresy emphasizing elaborate hidden mysteries and righteousness through works. We can only go forward safely in the Christian life if grace is with us.

Bibliography - Philippians & Colossians

Barclay, William *The Letters to the Philippians, Colossians, and Thessalonians* (Philadelphia: The Westminster Press, 1975)

Bruce, F.F. *The Epistles to the Colossians, to Philemon, and to the Ephesians* (Grand Rapids, Michigan: Eerdmans, 1988)

Clarke, Adam *The New Testament of Our Lord and Saviour Jesus Christ, Volume II* (New York: Eaton & Mains, 1832)

Dyke, Jeremiah *A Caveat for Archippus* (London: Harrison and Sons, 1898)

Erdman, Charles R. *The Epistles of Paul to the Colossians and to Philemon* (Grand Rapids, Michigan: Baker Books, 1983)

Kennedy, H.A.A. "The Epistle to the Philippians," *The Expositor's Greek Testament, Volume III* (London: Hodder and Stoughton Limited)

Kent, Homer A. Jr. "Philippians," *The Expositor's Bible Commentary, Volume 11* (Grand Rapids, Michigan: Zondervan, 1978)

Kirby, Jeremy B. *New Testament Overview - A Guide to Studying the New Testament and its Background* (Hannover, Calvary Books e.V., 2006)

Lane, W.L. "Ephesians-2 Thessalonians," *Daily Bible Commentary, Romans-Revelation* (Philadelphia, A.J. Holman, 1977)

Lenski, R.C.H. *The Interpretation of St. Paul's Epistles to the Galatians, Ephesians, and Philippians* (Minneapolis, Minnesota: Augsburg Publishing House, 1966)

Lightfoot, J.B. *St. Paul's Epistles to the Colossians and to Philemon* (Lynn, Massachusetts: Hendrickson Publishers, 1982)

Lightfoot, J.B. *St. Paul's Epistle to the Philippians* (Lynn, Massachusetts: Hendrickson Publishers, 1982)

Maclaren, *Alexander Expositions of Holy Scripture, Volumes 14 and 15* (Grand Rapids: Baker, 1984)

Martin, Ralph P. *The Epistle of Paul to the Philippians, An Introduction and Commentary* (Leicester, England: Inter-Varsity Press, 1987)

Meyer, F.B. *Our Daily Homily* (Westwood, New Jersey: Revell, 1966)

Morgan, G. Campbell *An Exposition of the Whole Bible* (Old Tappan, New Jersey: Revell, 1959)

Morgan, G. Campbell *Searchlights from the Word* (New York: Revell, 1926)

Mueller, Jac. J. *The Epistle of Paul to the Philippians* (Grand Rapids, Michigan: Eerdmans, 1988)

Peake, A.S. "The Epistle to the Colossians," *The Expositor's Greek Testament, Volume III* (London: Hodder and Stoughton Limited)

Poole, Matthew *A Commentary on the Holy Bible, Volume III: Matthew-Revelation* (London: Banner of Truth Trust, 1969, first published in 1685)

Robertson, A.T. *Word Pictures in the New Testament, Volume 4: Epistles of Paul* (Nashville: Broadman Press: 1933)

Spurgeon, Charles Haddon *The New Park Street Pulpit, Volumes 1-6* and *The Metropolitan Tabernacle Pulpit, Volumes 7-63* (Pasadena, Texas: Pilgrim Publications, 1990)

Trapp, John *A Commentary on the Old and New Testaments, Volume Five* (Eureka, California: Tanski Publications, 1997)

Vaughan, Curtis "Colossians" *The Expositor's Bible Commentary, Volume 11* (Grand Rapids, Michigan: Zondervan, 1978)

Vincent, Marvin R. *Word Studies in the New Testament, Volume III - The Epistles of Paul* (McLean, Virginia: MacDonald Publishing)

Wiersbe, Warren W. *The Bible Exposition Commentary, Volume 2* (Wheaton, Illinois: Victor Books, 1989)

Wright, N.T. *The Epistles of Paul to the Colossians and to Philemon, An Introduction and Commentary* (Leicester, England: Inter-Varsity Press, 1986)

Wuest, Kenneth S. *Wuest's Word Studies in the Greek New Testament, Volumes 1 and 2* (Grand Rapids, Michigan: Eerdmans, 1983)

As the years pass I love the work of studying, learning, and teaching the Bible more than ever. I'm so grateful that God is faithful to meet me in His Word.

I am very happy to dedicate this book to my oldest sister, Jan Guzik. Jan is the best kind of sister, citizen, follower of Jesus, and friend.

Once again I am in grateful debt to the proofreading and editorial help of Martina Patrick. Thanks to Annie Johnson for her help in preparing this commentary. Thanks also to Brian Procedo for the cover design and all the graphics work.

Most especially, thanks to my wife Inga-Lill. She is my loved and valued partner in life and in service to God and His people.

David Guzik

David Guzik's Bible commentary is regularly used and trusted by many thousands who want to know the Bible better. Pastors, teachers, class leaders, and everyday Christians find his commentary helpful for their own understanding and explanation of the Bible. David and his wife Inga-Lill live in Santa Barbara, California.

You can email David at
david@enduringword.com

For more resources by David Guzik,
go to www.enduringword.com